The
Morality
of Money

Biblical Roads to Financial Freedom

by

Ken Hubbard and Nick Pagano

McDougal Publishing is a ministry of The McDougal Foundation, Inc., a
Maryland nonprofit corporation dedicated to spreading the Gospel of the
Lord Jesus Christ to as many people as possible in the shortest
time possible.

Published by:

McDougal Publishing
P.O. Box 3595
Hagerstown, MD 21742-3595
www.mcdougalpublishing.com

ISBN 1-58158-076-2

Printed in the United States of America
For Worldwide Distribution

ENDORSEMENTS

Our checkbook and credit card statements reveal the true priorities in our lives. In a single, powerful volume, Ken Hubbard and Nick Pagano reveal the morality of money and proven principles to get us and keep us on the path to financial independence. If you plan to pass on to future generations a worthy inheritance, then The Morality of Money *is a must read in these changing times.*

— Dr. James O. Davis
Cofounder/President/CEO, Global Pastors Network

It's often said that money is the single most discussed topic throughout the entire Bible. Perhaps the reason so much attention is paid towards money is the tremendous impact it has over each of us throughout our lifetimes. The Morality of Money *explains and illustrates basic principles and lessons from the Bible in an extremely reader friendly format and in a manner that will surely change your life.*

— Mark G. Pollock
Partner and CEO, The Financial Group LCC

The Morality of Money *should be required reading for every pastor and church officer. It should be a part of the training of all communicants as well. It is the best treatise on the basics of financial planning that I have ever read. It could be the answer for many who are headed for financial problems. God has led these two committed Christians to do a valuable service.*

— Gordon Heffern
Former Chairman and CEO, Society Corporation
Cleveland, Ohio

Money is a tool to be used in God's service. Ken Hubbard and Nick Pagano show us how, demonstrating that, when it comes to money, attitude is far more important than amount. This book is a worthy investment and a profitable purchase for anyone trying to make sense of their money mess.

— Rex M. Rogers
President, Cornerstone University
Grand Rapids, Michigan

The Morality of Money *is a tremendous amount of basic information for everyone trying to improve their financial situation. Here you will find a concise coordination of principles and practices, especially on debt-free living.*

— Dr. Bruce Kresge
Retired family practioner

A simple, fun, Christian approach to a necessity of life—MONEY! I loved it!

— Billy "BD" Downs
Founder, BD's Mongolian Barbeque Restaurants

Christians often walk a fine line when it comes to understanding the role of money in their faith walk with the Lord Jesus Christ. For some, wealth indicates great faith, while for others, it is a sign of excess and a lack of spirituality. However, Ken and Nick present with biblical integrity the truth about money. They outline the practical steps to manage it properly for the benefit of both our lives and for those who will follow us.

— Greg Williams
President, Vanguard Creative Group
Chairman, Michigan Theological Seminary

Contents

PREFACE

When my friend and pastor, Ken Hubbard, and I first talked about coauthoring a book, I had to stop and muse about how far I had come in the realm of our book's topic. My first recollection of money is that some families had it and some did not. We were in the "did not" category. As I got older, I started to wonder why this happened and came to the conclusion that it was luck, or an inheritance, or fate, but I realize now that there are principles that relate to money just as there are principles for health, education, and the like.

My background is very similar to that of most other baby boomers. I grew up in a large Catholic family, and I remember the Kennedy assassination like it was yesterday. In high school, I accepted the Lord at a Fellowship of Christian Athletes function. I went on to college and tried to excel because getting a good job with a good company was the tried and true goal of every young person my age. In my first year out of college, I was a management trainee for a restaurant chain. I earned $10,400 a year (not bad in 1978). I remember the joy and excitement of making that much money because I had never made that much before. After a short time (one or two paychecks, probably), I realized that my take-home pay was a lot different from the salary I earned. My answer to making up the difference was to work harder to earn more. I figured $13,000 to $14,000 would do it and I would have it made. One thing led to another and I did make that unimaginable amount. After a short time, I realized that even that much was not enough and felt like I needed to make a little more to get ahead and figured I needed $18,000, then $25,000, then $40,000, then $60,000, then $100,000, then $150,000....

The first solution I came up with was more education. So, I went back to school to get my MBA. I had convinced myself that was the answer. Two years later and a few more dollars in debt, I headed out to conquer the world with my new degree in hand. At my first job, I received seven promotions in four years—I thought I finally had it made. But when my wife and I decided to start a family, we began wondering if the money we were making was really enough.

The second solution I came up with was to change my paradigm and go after bigger, better-paying jobs. As a result, I was constantly on the lookout for the "perfect" job. I never stopped to think that I wasn't the perfect employee. In a period of six years, I had six jobs—four were a result of my choice and two were the result of companies deciding that they no longer needed my services. Needless to say, there was instability and uncertainty on the home front. Looking back, I can see that neither of those two states are fruits of the Spirit, but it never dawned on me at the time.

I was constantly looking at our financial situation and asking why "it" wasn't working. I was doing everything I was supposed to (or so I thought). I was there early, had a positive attitude, dressed for success, and, on top of all that, I was a Christian. I started to question because, although I was making "a lot" of money, I could not get ahead of the financial power curve. It seemed that even though we made more money, we were broke at a higher level. After some thought and prayer, I decided to try my hand at starting my own company—and disaster struck! I launched the company, took in a partner, a man who was supposedly also a Christian, and crashed hard when this partner subsequently took all the money and disappeared into the night. This led to a serious evaluation of my faith and relationship with God because, in my own mind, I was "doing everything right" and still being punished. I had adopted the "Why me, God?" mentality. Many sleepless nights followed, along with making house payments on credit cards and trying to stay ahead of bill collectors. I remember one time when I even switched our long distance service so that I could cash a check and pay for groceries and diapers.

The lessons I learned were almost too numerous to mention. What finally brought me out of this tailspin? One of the first people I spoke with after getting over the embarrassment was a gentleman I knew who ran a local bank. When I told him of the embezzlement, he gave me an invaluable principle in two short words: "So what?" He went on to explain that everyone who makes a lot of money takes risks and most have losses. Those words were much more valuable than anything else he could have said or done. They set my perspective right again. I learned from my hard knocks and gained some insights that helped to set a more sure course for me and my family.

It is my and Ken's hope that this book can offer you some of the insights and principles we've learned in the school of hard knocks. Perhaps you've read my story thinking that I was pretty well off because I had nice houses and new cars. Or perhaps success to you is simply having a working vehicle and a roof over your head. Either case could be true or false, because real success doesn't lie in what you have or don't have. One man may have few material possessions and be living an abundant life, while another man who has all the wealth imaginable may feel like a failure because his wife is distant and his kids no longer know him. Success is really a journey, not a destination. God has created *all of us* to be successful—to have an abundant life.

I am often asked how I got out of the difficult situations in my life in order for us to be where we are today. This book contains the answer. A review of biblical principles shows us that everyone in biblical history had issues to face. Joseph's family threw him into a pit. David's family belittled him, and his best friend's father tried numerous times to kill him. Paul was shipwrecked, jailed, and persecuted. Nehemiah faced challenges from outsiders as he directed the rebuilding of Jerusalem's walls. Why would I have the audacity to think that God would make *my* life a bed of roses?

I share all of this with you, not because I am proud of my "stupid period" (as my wife calls it), but because I see a lot of other people going through the same battles. It is my belief that many of us go through the school of hard knocks as it relates to our finances. The challenge is to learn from those times and to not make the same mistakes over and over. This project is my attempt to give something back to God and maybe to save one family from going through what we had to experience.

When one undertakes a project like this, there are many who deserve credit and acknowledgment. First, I want to recognize my wife and sons, my parents, and my siblings for providing support and motivation to dream big dreams.

Second, as Solomon wrote in Ecclesiastes, "There is nothing new under the sun." I want to acknowledge and thank many of my mentors, some of whom I know and some whom I have never met. I learned from Turner Thompson that you can reach the top even if you start below the bottom. I learned from Brad Doyle that success is not an accident. I learned from Joe Brooks that financial success comes from building a plan and sticking to it. I learned life-changing information from Robert Kiyosaki, Paul Zane Pilzer, Brian Tracy, and a host of others whom I have never had the privilege of meeting.

Finally, I want to acknowledge and thank my friend, pastor, and co-author, Ken Hubbard, who taught me that God really does care about everything we do—so we should do it with excellence.

— Nick Pagano

I, too, would like to thank the many mentors I have learned from through their books, seminars and teachings though I've never had the privilege of meeting them. Larry Burkett, T.D. Jakes and countless others whom I have listened to over the years have sown into my life and have shaped my philosophies. Anyone who proclaims to be a self-made man hasn't made much of his man, but thanks to all of you, I am a better man because of you and your teachings.

— Ken Hubbard

INTRODUCTION

Money—while some never mention it, others think and talk of little else. Some have fanciful dreams of winning the lottery and having no concerns (financial or otherwise) for the rest of their lives. Others dread losing a portion of a multimillion-dollar portfolio. Still others lie awake at night wondering if they can feed their kids or pay their rent. Regardless of our present situation and perspective, all of us agree that money is a constant in our lives.

For all of us, our financial knowledge and perspective is the result of what we have learned and experienced over time. Our financial instructors have been our parents, pastors, teachers, bosses, mentors, and friends. We go through life building upon this foundation, or lack thereof, whether we are consciously aware of it or not.

Regardless of our present knowledge and situation, there is room for improvement. The individual who has wealth and knowledge has as much room to learn and grow as does the individual who has no wealth or financial knowledge. How is this paradox possible?

Today, many of us do not have the proper understanding of God's financial principles, which leads to financial hardships for our children and ourselves. Presently, debt is not only expected, it is normal, yet it strangles individuals, businesses, careers, and families. How is it that we live in a land and a time with more of everything material yet have more bankruptcies?

People are asking, "How can I get more? How much is enough? Is there such a thing as good debt? How much do I need to retire? How come it always seems that we have more month than money?"

The questions are endless, but require answers nonetheless. But having all the knowledge does not by itself resolve the issue. The answer lies in having knowledge in conjunction with a change in behavior. That is the foundation of this book—finding answers and behaviors that will be of practical benefit to each of us and to those we in turn will instruct.

We look around and see our neighbors and friends who appear to have significantly more money and signficantly less financial stress than we have and we wonder why. Why is it that some families seem to have an endless supply of money and we never seem to have enough to cover the basics? Are there secrets to financial success that some know and we don't?

Money impacts our daily lives. Money, or lack thereof, impacts most facets of our lives: the houses we live in, the cars we drive, the places we vacation, the schools our kids attend, our health care, etc. But many of us know very little about it. There are very few classes (if any) on personal finance in the school system, so we have learned what we know from our friends and neighbors, the school of hard knocks, professionals, or on our own.

Most Americans handle their money the same way their parents did. They, in turn, teach their children the same methods, routines, and habits they learned. Indeed, our experience has shown that people who own stocks have parents who did. People who have all their money in CDs usually have parents who did also. Even if previous generations were successful financially, we cannot always follow closely in their footsteps. While our parents and grandparents paid relatively little in taxes, today we lose more than one third of our income to Uncle Sam. Institutions such as Social Security and corporate pensions have questionable futures. People are living longer and saving less. Americans need to recognize, like never before, that they are responsible for their own financial futures. And yet, many of us are financially ignorant.

The Bible records an interesting story about David in 1 Samuel 22. David was fleeing Saul and came to the cave of Adullam just after his insanity act before King Achish. In verse 2 of that chapter, we read, "All those who were in distress or in debt or discontented gathered around him, and he became their leader." Maybe this instance was the beginning of the saying "Misery loves company." Unfortunately, the situation is reminiscent of a large percentage of the Body of Christ today. We are in distress, in debt, and discontented. The three D's are related. One could argue which one causes which, but we think we all have felt the emotional burden of debt and realize it can cause us to be distressed and discontented.

This book is for people who have felt and lived that way. It is for those who get confused by all the numbers in *The Wall Street Journal*, have never read a book on economic theory, or haven't read the latest articles on personal finances. This book is designed to provide information in a commonsense manner—not in a jargon-filled, dumbed-down, condemning, or esoteric manner. We don't wear green eyeshades or pocket protectors. All we have done is combine real-life experiences of two men, one with a business focus and the other with a pastoral focus. It is our hope and prayer that you can learn from our mistakes rather than make your own. In so doing, we hope you will experience more personal prosperity and less stress, and be in a position to provide greater financial assistance to your local church.

CHAPTER ONE

THE FOUR R'S

Today, there are few taboo subjects left in the church. It seems we can talk about anything under the sun, even private or sensitive subjects of the type that would have made our parents blush just a generation ago. Such openness can be good in that it fosters honest discussion and communication which can lead to understanding and healing.

Some subjects, however, still make many Christians uncomfortable. Money is one of them. For some reason, we just don't like to talk about financial matters in church, particularly when the discussion begins to get personal. It's okay for the pastor to talk about tithing during the annual stewardship campaign; after all, that's expected. But just let him mention money from the pulpit any other time of the year, and people start squirming in their pews and getting a firm grip on their wallets and pocketbooks. The moment he steps outside the bounds of the tithe to talk about personal money matters is when folks start thinking, "Ah, Pastor, watch out! You've gone from preachin' to meddlin'!"

It's as though we believe that talking about financial matters in church is somehow unspiritual. We would much rather spend our time in Bible study and in praise and worship, singing and shouting and celebrating together before the Lord. After all, isn't that much more fun than discussing mundane matters such as money? At the same time, however, why is it that so many Christians who joyfully speak of the God who "will meet all [their] needs according to his glorious riches in Christ Jesus" (Philippians 4:19) cannot pay their bills from month to month? Why is it that in this age of affluence there are so many churches that don't have two cents to rub together to fund needed ministries? Why is it that churches that do have a lot of money so often spend millions on their own infrastructure while evangelism, missions, and community-focused outreach ministries go begging?

Clearly, something is amiss.

Part of the problem lies with our own attitude. Contrary to what many of us think, the subject of finances is a highly spiritual issue. Of the thirty-eight parables of Jesus recorded in the four gospels, sixteen deal with money or money management. Judging from the gospels, Jesus spent more time in His public ministry talking about money and finances than any other single subject. The New Testament as a whole has more to say about money than about Heaven and hell combined.

If the Word of God places this much importance on financial matters, then we would do well to do the same. Many churches and individual Christians suffer from ignorance and false or faulty teaching on the subject of money. The result oftentimes is the spectacle of the children of the King begging bread before a skeptical world that desperately needs to know the God who truly is sufficient for all their needs, spiritual or otherwise. It is time for we in the church to unstop our ears and take our blinders off when it comes to matters of money. We can no longer afford to think of the subject of finances as "unspiritual." The time has come for us to replace our ignorance and false ideas with wisdom and knowledge.

Jesus gave the Church a great mission when He said, "…go and make disciples of all nations, baptizing them in the name of the Father and of the Son and of the Holy Spirit, and teaching them to obey everything I have commanded you" (Matthew 28:19-20a). The Lord never gives an assignment without providing the resources necessary for its success. Every mission requires money. Who will finance the mission of the Church if it is not the saints? How can we finance the mission of the Church if we are ignorant of money matters and basic principles of financial management?

God's people perish for lack of understanding, and our mission is in jeopardy. Proverbs 29:18 says, "Where there is no revelation, the people cast off restraint; but blessed is he who keeps the law." As the saints of God, we need revelation regarding financial matters so that our dreams in the Lord can be realized and our mission accomplished. Every dream needs money and will die without it. Too many churches and too many saints are bound to the empty shells of dead dreams, dreams that were killed by ignorance or false teaching.

We must not allow our mission to be compromised. Our message must not be silenced by the screaming voice of lack and need. The time for ignorance is past. It is time for us to go to school on the matter of finances and money management for Christian believers and their churches. Just as schools of old taught the three R's—readin', 'ritin', and 'rithmatic—we need first to learn the four R's of finances: the *root*, the *rut*, the *rich*, and the *reward*.

The Root

The first thing we have to do is get rid of the notion that money is evil. Money is neither good nor bad; it is what we *do* with money that makes it either one or the other. You can use the same $100.00 to buy crack or to buy groceries for a week. Money is a commodity that can be utilized for either good or evil purposes. It is, therefore, morally neutral.

Many people have bought into the lie that money makes you a better person. In reality, money merely enhances or illuminates the person you already are. People who have money are not necessarily evil, nor are people without money automatically good. Goodness and evil are qualities of character. Money is simply a vehicle that brings to light the character that already drives us. Whether we are good or evil will be revealed in our attitude toward money and in how we use it. What we do with money reveals what is important to us. We can be greedy with a hundred dollars or with a million dollars.

Money can drive us either away from God or to God. After all, money is not the problem. The problem is *love* of money. Some people claim that "money is the root of all evil." This is a misconception based on a misquoting of Scripture. When the apostle Paul wrote to Timothy, his young protégé in the ministry, he included some wise counsel regarding our attitude toward money and worldly possessions:

> *If anyone teaches false doctrines and does not agree to the sound instruction of our Lord Jesus Christ and to godly teaching, he is conceited and understands nothing. He has an unhealthy interest in controversies and quarrels about words that result in envy, strife, malicious talk, evil suspicions and constant friction between men of corrupt mind, who have been robbed of the truth and who think that godliness is a means to financial gain. But godliness with contentment is great gain. For we brought nothing into the world, and we can take nothing out of it. But if we have food and clothing, we will be content with that. People who want to get rich fall into temptation and a trap and into many foolish and harmful desires that plunge men into ruin and destruction. For the love of money is a root of all kinds of evil. Some people, eager for money, have wandered from the faith and pierced themselves with many griefs. But you, man of God, flee from all this, and pursue righteousness, godliness, faith, love, endurance and gentleness. Fight the good fight of the faith. Take hold of the eternal life to which you were called when you made your good confession in the presence of many witnesses.*
>
> 1 Timothy 6:3-12

As Paul makes clear in verse 10, money itself is not the problem, but "the *love* of money" is a root of all kinds of evil. In other words, if money and the pursuit of wealth are the driving force in our lives, we are headed for trouble. Although this verse is the central thrust of this passage, Paul has some other important things to say as well. Let's look a little closer at them.

First of all, Paul had to deal with some of the same issues about financial false teaching that we face today. In verses 3-5 he refers to "men of corrupt mind" who were "conceited" and without understanding, teaching "false doctrines" that did not agree with "sound instruction" and "godly teaching." These false teachers were deceived—and were deceiving others—into believing that "godliness is a means to *financial gain*." In other words, their motive for preaching, teaching, and following Christ was for what they could get out of it financially.

Today we contend with many different teachings on finances in the Church that are just plain wrong. One of these is misuse and abuse of the "Give and it shall be given" principle: "Give, and it will be given to you. A good measure, pressed down, shaken together and running over, will be poured into your lap. For with the measure you use, it will be measured to you" (Luke 6:38). While the principle itself is certainly true, *motivation* makes all the difference. If the only reason we give is so we can receive, we are in error.

Another false teaching prevalent in much of the Church is the belief that poverty is "spiritual." In other words, the poorer we are, the closer to God we are. At the other end of the spectrum, but just as misguided, is the belief that great abundance is "spiritual." According to this idea, the more faith we exercise, the more God will bless us with material abundance. While there is nothing inherently wrong with having money, there is nothing sinful about being poor, either. In some ways it takes more faith to be poor than to be prosperous. Just having less than someone else does not mean you are less "spiritual."

As a counter to the false idea that godliness is a means to financial gain, Paul says in verse 6 that "godliness with contentment is great gain." In the business and financial worlds, another word for "gain" is "profit." God wants us to turn a profit. He created us to be profitable (which does not necessarily mean having a lot of money) and wants to see us fulfill our potential. Profit in life comes through learning contentment: in other words, not continually lusting for more, more, more. Too many Christians get caught up, financing their *wants,* then praying for their *needs* when they are out of money. Then they are puzzled when God does not answer. *God won't support poor stewardship.*

Anything material in nature we should hold with a light grip, "For we brought nothing into the world, and we can take nothing out of it" (verse 7). Think about it: have you ever seen a hearse pulling a U-Haul trailer? No matter what we attain or acquire in this life, we can't take it with us. Nothing tangible is eternal. That is why Jesus said, "Do not store up for yourselves treasures on earth, where moth and rust destroy, and where thieves break in and steal. But store up for yourselves treasures in heaven, where moth and rust do not destroy, and where thieves do not break in and steal. For where your treasure is, there your heart will be also" (Matthew 6:19-21). Earthly treasures will pass away. Only the treasure we store up in Heaven will last.

Paul strikes the contentment theme again in verse 8: "But if we have food and clothing, we will be content with that." The bottom line is that we must learn to be content at whatever level, knowing that God has promised to supply all our *needs*. Anything beyond that is icing on the cake. In this, Paul was speaking from his own experience:

> *I rejoice greatly in the Lord that at last you have renewed your concern for me. Indeed, you have been concerned, but you had no opportunity to show it. I am not saying this because I am in need, for I have learned to be content whatever the circumstances. I know what it is to be in need, and I know what it is to have plenty. I have learned the secret of being content in any and every situation, whether well fed or hungry, whether living in plenty or in want. I can do everything through him who gives me strength.* Philippians 4:10-13

Contentment is critical to success and prosperity in every area of life because if we cannot thank God at our present level, we will never rise to the next level. God invests in those who are faithful. As we prove ourselves faithful in small things, He will entrust us with greater things.

In 1 Timothy 6:9, Paul is not speaking against being rich but against pursuing wealth for its own sake or as the driving force in one's life. The drive for wealth is a "temptation" that traps people into "foolish and harmful desires," resulting in "ruin and destruction." If being rich becomes your primary goal in life, then it becomes your god. Pursuit of your "god" of wealth will drive you away from the God of truth and life. If the pursuit of wealth becomes your god, then eventually any method to attain it, no matter how shady, will become acceptable.

Paul finally arrives at the central theme of the passage in verse 10: "For the love of money is a root of all kinds of evil. Some people, eager for money, have wandered from the faith and pierced themselves with many griefs." What is the *root* of all kinds of evil? The *love* of money. How much money you have makes no difference. Little or much, if the *love* of money rules your heart, you are in trouble.

Take a personal inventory of your heart. Are you obsessed with money? Before you answer, think about this: loving *anything* more than God is a sin. Do you think about making money more than you think about pursuing God? When you do seek to make money, do you seek it for your own self-benefit or to benefit the Kingdom of God?

Consider the Good Samaritan (see Luke 10:30-37). He had money, but his money did not have him. Money was a tool, a commodity to be used to benefit others, in this case, a man who had been beaten and robbed by thieves. This Samaritan gave willingly and liberally out of his own abundance to help a stranger in need.

God will allow no rivals. He will not share His glory or sovereignty with anyone else: "'If you do not listen, and if you do not set your heart to honor my name,' says the Lord Almighty, 'I will send a curse upon you, and I will curse your blessings. Yes, I have already cursed them, because you have not set your heart to honor me'" (Malachi 2:2). One reason so many Christians have financial problems is because they have not honored God with the resources He has blessed them with, and those blessings have become curses.

If we are not to pursue wealth as the driving force of our lives, what *are* we to pursue? Paul gives the answer in 1 Timothy 6:11: "But you, man of God, flee from all this, and pursue righteousness, godliness, faith, love, endurance and gentleness." These are intangible qualities, but they last forever. Why pour blood, toil, tears, and sweat into things that will pass away in a lifetime?

Proof of desire is in the pursuit. How many of us will seriously go after something we don't really want? What desires control your heart? What do you spend your money on? What do you devote your time to? Let me glance at your daytimer calendar and your checkbook and I can tell you where your treasure is.

The *love* of money is the *root* of all kinds of evil. What then is the *root* of success in every area of life, finances included? There is no better answer to this question than the words of Jesus: "But seek first his kingdom and his righteousness, and all these things will be given to you as well" (Matthew 6:33).

The Rut

When we speak of a "rut" as one of the four R's of finances, we are referring to the poverty mindset that traps so many people, including many Christian believers, and holds them in bondage to financial insufficiency. This is the attitude that says, "I am poor, I have always been poor, and I will always be poor; that's just the way things are," or "My parents were poor, my grandparents were poor, so I will be poor also."

Such thinking is a dangerous "rut" that is easy to get into but very difficult to get out of. A Canadian road sign at a wilderness crossroads said, "Be careful which ruts you pick; you will be in them a long time." Someone once said that a rut is a grave with the ends kicked out. Another saying we've heard is that the difference between a rut and a grave is the depth of the hole and the length of the stay. There is a lot of truth to both statements, especially when it comes to finances. The rut of poverty can kill our hopes and our dreams and any confidence we may once have had of ever achieving anything better.

Such a poverty mindset affects not only individual believers, but can infect entire churches, which rationalize it by cloaking it in spiritual terminology. Generally speaking, financial attitudes in the Church often tend toward one or the other of two extremes: poverty = spirituality or abundance = spirituality. The truth lies somewhere in the middle in a balance between the two: balance = spirituality. Just as a balanced diet promotes optimal physical health, so a balanced attitude toward money and its place in our lives promotes optimal financial health.

So then, where did this *rut* of a poverty mindset come from? How did it get started and how has it gained such a foothold in the minds of so many believers and in the practices of so many churches? Let me share from my own experience.

We both grew up in poor neighborhoods. During our childhood and our youth we never learned anything about wealth or financial management, and nobody in our neighborhoods knew anything about them either. We were all poor together and that was that. Poor neighborhoods usually have poor churches that justify their lack by declaring it "spiritual": "We are spiritual because we are serving the Lord and doing His work in spite of our lack of resources. Money would only tempt us and turn us away from Him."

All of us have the human tendency to criticize those who are different—and particularly, opposite—from the way we are. The poor condemn the rich as people who cannot possibly love God because of all their money. As proof, they point to Jesus' statement that it is easier for a camel to go through the eye of a needle than for a rich man to enter the Kingdom of God (see Matthew 19:24). At the same time, the poor console themselves by singing, "I have a mansion over the hilltop." The rich, on the other hand, condemn the poor for their poverty, saying that they need to be more "spiritual" like the wealthy Jews in the Bible. For their part, they point to people like Abraham, Jacob, Solomon, Nicodemus, and Joseph of Arimathea as examples.

How do we solve this dilemma? The answer is *balance*—both sides coming together to help each other in mutual respect and Christian brotherly love.

The rut of the poverty mindset began with men trying to separate themselves from the things of this world. This philosophy of asceticism is taught and practiced not only in Christianity but also in Buddhism, Hinduism, and many other world religions. Behind the practice lies the belief that the more we can separate ourselves from the material world, the more we can attain deeper spirituality.

Such separation from the things of the world is noble and even biblical—to a point. Jesus said that no one can serve two masters. Either we serve God or we serve money; we cannot serve both. James 4:4 warns, "You adulterous people, don't you know that friendship with the world is hatred toward God? Anyone who chooses to be a friend of the world becomes an enemy of God." In 1 John 2:15, the Word explicitly states, "Do not love the world or anything in the world. If anyone loves the world, the love of the Father is not in him."

Anything taken to an extreme is unhealthy. Separation from the world in order to stay focused on God is one thing. It is a physical means to a spiritual end. Outright rejection of money and wealth is another thing entirely because it makes separation an end in itself, elevates poverty to a lofty spiritual plane that it does not deserve, and bankrupts the Church from carrying out its mission. Money is a tool, a commodity, a vehicle—a medium of exchange that is necessary in our world to get things done. We need an attitude shift when it comes to money.

During the Great Depression, it was easy to criticize wealth because nobody had any. The message of poverty became very palatable, especially in the churches, because it consoled people in their lack. Eventually, we became stuck in a "theology of poverty" that said that jewelry was out and fine clothing was vanity because nobody had money to spend on those kinds of things. Over time, the attitude that said, "We *cannot* spend money on those things" evolved into "We *should not* spend money on those things." We adopted a teaching from an era that had nothing and therefore found it easy to criticize wealth and abundance.

As our national and global economy changed and improved, our attitude and teaching about money and wealth basically stayed the same. As a result, many Christians and churches even today are caught in the rut of poverty thinking. While business owners, professional sports figures, drug dealers, and hard-working Americans of all kinds—believers and nonbelievers alike—continue to make and accumulate money and wealth, many Christians still believe money is evil. Churches reconcile themselves to not having enough money or other resources to carry out their ministries and assume this is the way things are supposed to be. One sad result is a diminished view of God among many believers, a view that sees God as either unwilling or unable to provide adequately for His people in the midst of a hostile and godless world.

As Christians, we are children of the King and yet we can't pay our bills or afford to fund the ministries of our church. Something is terribly wrong with this picture! We should be financially solvent and self-sufficient—wealthy even, perhaps—not for our own sake or selfish pleasure but to use it for the advancement of God's Kingdom and His purposes on earth. In other words, we should be blessed so that we can be a blessing. We are only pilgrims passing through, but while we are passing through, we need to be able to build bigger vehicles so others can pass through with us!

God created us to be successful. He told Adam and Eve to be fruitful and to multiply, and to replenish, subdue, and exercise dominion over the earth. Those are characteristics of success. Later, in Jeremiah 29:11, He promised, "For I know the plans I have for you...plans to prosper you and not to harm you, plans to give you hope and a future." In Romans 8:37, Paul says that we are "more than conquerors" through Christ who loved us.

God's plan and desire for us is that we be prosperous and successful. We're not saying that every Christian should be rich, but let's not make a blanket statement either that it is wrong to have money or wealth. It may not be God's plan for every Christian to be wealthy in this world, but neither is it His plan for any of His children to be stuck in the rut of poverty, unable to pay their bills or get ahead. Late in his life, David the psalmist wrote, "I was young and now I am old, yet I have never seen the righteous forsaken or their children begging bread" (Psalm 37:25).

Likewise, the Church should be able to write its own ticket in the world, rather than be the poor stepsister dependent on handouts and the benevolence of others. Individually and collectively, it is time for us to renovate our thinking and get ourselves and our churches out of the rut of poverty thinking.

The Rich

At the other end of the spectrum is the philosophy that says if you do not have everything you need—and more—then you do not have enough faith. People with this mindset believe and teach that our faith is demonstrated through what we *have*. In their view, the greater our faith, the more we will have. Consequently, according to this misguided teaching, people who have little also have small faith. We would suggest that it is really the other way around. It takes *more* faith to live without than to live with.

Central to the success of this philosophy is convincing people to give in order to get, using Luke 6:38 as justification: "Give, and it will be given to you. A good measure, pressed down, shaken together and running over, will be poured into your lap. For with the measure you use, it will be measured to you." From this perspective, giving and faith are interrelated: If we do not give, we do not have faith. The more faith we have, the more we will give. The more we give, the more faith we demonstrate.

While this relationship between faith and giving is correct as far as it goes, we must also be careful to live by *all* of God's prescribed principles and promises. We can give—and should—but in order to prosper and advance in life we also must work, turn a profit, and invest some of our return for the future. Our faith will work *if we work it!*

God gives us the ability to produce wealth, but we have to produce it. He provides prosperity, but we have to go after it. When the Israelites were living in the wilderness after leaving Egypt, God provided manna to sustain them, but *they* had to go out daily and gather it. By leading them across the Jordan into Canaan, God gave the Israelites a land flowing with milk and honey, just as He had promised since the days of Abraham, but *they* had to work and go to war against heathen enemies in order to possess and settle it.

In faith and finances, just as in every other area of life, there is no free lunch and no getting rich quick. God will provide wealth, but we must exercise discipline and faithfulness in financial planning, wise stewardship, investing, tithes, and offerings. Our goal should never be how wealthy we can be but how well we can be.

Somehow we must destroy the myth that if we drive a nicer car than someone else, we have more faith than they do, and more of the favor of God. Those who follow this philosophy of faith preaching on wealth believe that poverty is the result of sin. This is the same error that many people in Jesus' day made. Then, as now, many believed that poor people were sinners under God's wrath and judgment and rich people were His special favorites and enjoyed His favor. On more than one occasion Jesus addressed that error and tried to correct it in the minds of His disciples and others who heard Him.

Although we believe that poverty is a curse that should be broken, we do not believe that poverty is always a result of sin. Sometimes poverty is simply a mindset that has been passed from one generation to the next and will continue to do so until it is deliberately broken. Just because one person may have a bigger house than you does not mean he is more spiritual than you or more in favor with God. Not everyone wants or needs a big house.

The size of our bank account and the amount of "stuff" we have are not reliable indicators of the level of our faith. We will not all be at the same level financially for many reasons: educational level, job skills, chosen vocation or profession. For some, the nature of God's call on their lives will preclude significant material or financial prosperity. For others, immaturity and irresponsibility will limit how far they can go. God simply cannot entrust everyone with wealth. He plays the stock market. God will invest heavily in those who have demonstrated their ability to bring a good return, but only lightly in those who have not. This is the point of Jesus' parable of the three servants (or investors) in the Matthew chapter 25, which we will consider in greater detail later.

When Jesus said that we should lay up for ourselves treasures in Heaven, He was saying that we should invest only in things that will last—things that will appreciate in value. This is important because the wealth we build is not for us alone but also for those in need around us as well as those who will follow after us. Material prosperity means little without a disciplined faith walk with the Lord. The Laodicean church of Revelation 3:14-22 was materially wealthy but spiritually bankrupt. Their physical prosperity had blinded them to the smallness of their faith, and the Lord threatened to spit them out of His mouth because they were only lukewarm.

If the Church cannot lead by example in matters of prosperity—financial or otherwise—who will minister to the wealthy? Who will lead them to Christ and teach them how to invest their wealth in the Kingdom of God? How will we as children of the King learn to live accordingly, not wastefully or for our own self-pleasure, but responsibly and confidently as witnesses to the God of more than enough?

Such leadership requires someone who has "been there, done that." Although Moses was a great and effective leader, facing down Pharaoh and bringing the Israelites out of slavery in Egypt, he had spent most of his life in the desert. Moses could lead the children of Israel to the borders of the Promised Land, but he could not lead them in. He had never been there. It fell to Joshua, who had actually seen and walked in the land of Canaan as one of the twelve spies Moses had sent on a scouting mission, to actually lead the people in to take possession of their inheritance.

The Reward

In a sense, the plight of many Christians today who struggle to get by financially can be compared to that of the Israelites in Egypt. For example, both are in a form of bondage. We talk about many kinds of bondage in church—pornography, tobacco, alcohol, drugs—but rarely do we discuss *financial* bondage. Yet, probably more Christians are bound financially than are bound by any of the others. Under Pharaoh's hand, the Israelites were stuck in the *rut* of poverty. They had almost nothing they could call their own. Their situation worsened when Pharaoh commanded them to fetch their own straw for bricks and yet continue to produce the same number of bricks. Like the Israelites, Christians in financial bondage are caught in the *rut* of "not enough."

Believers caught in the faith/wealth "Give and it will be given" *rich* mindset are like the Israelites in the wilderness. Moses appeared, and by God's powerful hand delivered the children of Israel from slavery and took them to freedom in the desert. There God provided for their every need on a day-by-day basis. Now they were *rich*, receiving from God's hand not more than they needed, but just enough.

Finally, after forty years in the wilderness, Joshua led the children of Israel into the Promised Land where, after they had defeated the different people groups that were living there and had settled throughout Canaan, they came into their *reward*: self-sufficiency in the land. They had gone from the *rut* of "not enough" under Pharaoh's hand, to the *rich* of "just enough" under God's hand in the desert, to the *reward* of "more than enough" under their own hand, providing for themselves in the land flowing with milk and honey.

The odyssey of the Israelites from *rut* to *rich* to *reward* represents the journey we must take as Christians from financial bondage to financial freedom. Only when we free ourselves from the bondage of false financial teachings and assumptions by following God's principles of financial management will we be able to attain the prosperity God desires for us and realize the full potential—the "more than enough"—that He designed into us. Our understanding has become so skewed that we tend to think of insufficiency as the norm. To correct our understanding, we need to reexamine God's original design and intent.

Chapter Two

Created to Prosper

The world we live in runs on money. Money is the fuel that stokes the fires of commerce. Governments and businesses cannot survive without it. A nation's wealth is measured by its per capita income and its gross domestic product. It seems that more and more the "haves" call the shots, while the "have-nots" have little choice but to follow along. Everywhere, the "golden rule" applies: Those with the gold make the rules.

Let's face it: We all need money. As we saw in chapter one, money is morally neutral—neither good nor evil. It is a commodity, albeit a necessary one. We delude ourselves when we insist that money is not important. Just try paying your rent or your mortgage or your utility bill without money and see what happens! Try putting groceries on the table for your family without money and you will discover very quickly how important money is to daily life.

Money is important, but we must guard against the error of making money *all-important*. That is what the world as a whole has done, which is *one* reason why the world is in such a mess. Most of the people in the world, particularly in the highly industrialized nations, live for money. Although the Bible never condemns money or the making of money, it *does* condemn allowing money to become our god, our end-all and be-all. That is what Paul meant when he said that the *love* of money is the root of all kinds of evil. Anything we love supremely becomes "god" to us.

Like everything else in our fallen world, money and its uses have been corrupted by Satan and by human sin. What God meant for good, man has turned to evil and selfish purposes. While freedom and life characterize the Kingdom of God, our fallen world is characterized by bondage and death. Apart from Christ, we are all in bondage to sin, even "dead in [our] transgressions and sins" (Ephesians 2:1). We are enslaved by all kinds of addictions, whether tobacco, alcohol, drugs, sex, pornography, or the like. In addition, millions of us, including many, many Christians, are in *financial bondage*. Either we are controlled by the pursuit of wealth, or we are enslaved by the product of our credit-driven economy—a particularly insidious kind of bondage called *debt*.

It wasn't always this way. There was a time when bondage was unknown on the earth and everything worked exactly the way it was supposed to. In the beginning God created the heavens and the earth and everything on the earth, including all life. God saw that everything He had created was very good. He created man to rule over the created order in His name. When Adam and Eve sinned in the Garden of Eden, everything changed. Their nature and character were corrupted by sin, as was all the created order. Instead of rulers over the earth, men became slaves to their own lusts and passions, slaves to their sin and to Satan. Even man's attitude and understanding regarding finances and money was corrupted.

In order to understand money and financial matters properly, we need to look first at how things are *supposed* to work—how they *did* work in the beginning according to God's original design. God created man for freedom, not slavery. He created us to prosper, not to struggle day by day just to get by and subsist in an environment of insufficiency. We can see this in the fivefold mandate He gave to Adam and Eve at creation.

God's design and intention for man are found in the closing verses of Genesis chapter one. Although these verses do not specifically address financial matters, the principles still apply, since they cover all of life. Listen to what God said:

> *Then God said, "Let us make man in our image, in our likeness, and let them rule over the fish of the sea and the birds of the air, over the livestock, over all the earth, and over all the creatures*

that move along the ground." So God created man in his own
image, in the image of God he created him; male and female he
created them. God blessed them and said to them, "Be fruitful
and increase in number; fill the earth and subdue it. Rule over
the fish of the sea and the birds of the air and over every living
creature that moves on the ground" ...Now the Lord God had
planted a garden in the east, in Eden; and there he put the man
he had formed. ...The Lord God took the man and put him in
the Garden of Eden to work it and take care of it.

Genesis 1:26-28; 2:8, 15

When God created man, He made him ruler over the created order,
but it was not a passive rule. In addition, God gave man meaningful
work to do. Adam was to rule over the Garden of Eden and its inhabitants even as he took care of it on a day-by-day basis. Purposeful work
is essential to our sense of well-being and for giving meaning to our
lives. Fruitfulness is virtually impossible without it.

Our primary focus, however, is on the five commands that God gave
to Adam and Eve. Let's look at them again, as found in the King James
Version:

And God blessed them, and God said unto them, Be fruitful, and
multiply, and replenish the earth, and subdue it: and have
dominion over the fish of the sea, and over the fowl of the air,
and over every living thing that moveth upon the earth.

Genesis 1:28, KJV

In this passage of Scripture, God gave Adam and Eve five instructions:

1. Be fruitful
2. Multiply
3. Replenish the earth
4. Subdue the earth
5. Have dominion (rule) over all living things on the earth.

For our current purpose, we want to apply these commands to the
area of our finances. For any of you who may fear that we are taking
these scriptures out of context or misapplying them, let us just say

that God is interested in *every* area of our lives, and these principles apply to every area of life. Our Lord is just as concerned with our finances and our attitudes and practices regarding money as He is about other areas that we may consider more "spiritual." Otherwise, why would so many of the recorded words of Jesus in the four gospels be devoted to the subject?

With this in mind, let's examine each of these five commands in more detail.

Be Fruitful

God's first command to Adam and Eve was to "be fruitful." Scripture says that before God gave them any commands, He first blessed them. One of the wonderful things about God is that He never gives us a command without also giving us the means or the resources to carry it out. God *blessed* Adam and Eve. He placed a seed inside of them and then said, "Be fruitful."

Fruitfulness is impossible without a seed. We have to plant apple seeds if we ever hope to have any apples! Whenever God asks us to do something, we should consider it a compliment because it means that He knows we already have what it will take to accomplish the task. He knows because He put it there Himself. Inside each one of us reside the seeds for everything God desires for us.

Sometimes the seed is invisible to us. That's okay. If God commands us to do something, whether spiritually, financially, or any other way, we can rest assured that the seed is already in us, whether we can see it or not. Let's say, for example, that you hear an inspiring missionary speaker in church. After learning of the great needs that exist on the mission field you sense God saying to you, "Write a check for $300.00 to help meet those needs." You feel that neither your checking nor savings accounts can afford that kind of outlay. What do you do? If God has told you to write the check, *write the check*. He sees a seed that may be invisible to you. If you plant that seed in obedience and faith, God will bring a harvest back to you. At the time, you may not see where that harvest, or return, will come from or how it will happen, but God will see to it. We are not advocating financial irresponsibility here but responsiveness to the voice of the Lord. He will never require of you anything that He does not equip you to give.

Usually when we read this command to "be fruitful," we think of reproduction and making babies. While that is undoubtedly the central thought here, there are many other ways to be fruitful as well. We believe that God is commanding us today to be fruitful as Christians. If He wants us to be fruitful, that means that somewhere He has already invested in us. He has already put the seeds for our fruitfulness inside us.

In the beginning, God created us in His image. God made nothing into something. He is a creative God and we are made in His image. That means we are creative as well. Our creative Creator placed inside each of us a seed of creativity. It may be creativity in the arts, or teaching, or business, or music, or writing, or auto mechanics—something. Whatever your creative bent may be, God has also given you the ability to be successful at it. Deuteronomy 8:18 says, "But remember the Lord your God, for it is he who gives you the ability to produce wealth, and so confirms his covenant, which he swore to your forefathers, as it is today."

Just think about it: *God has put inside each of us the ability to produce wealth!* What an incredible thought! God designed us to be wealth-producers. He built into us the ability to use our inherent creativity to prosper and to reach our full potential. That's what fruitfulness is: fulfilling our design and purpose. What is the purpose of an apple tree? To produce apples. An apple tree that does not produce apples may look pretty to the eye with its thick branches and lush green leaves, but it has failed in its designed purpose.

What has God put inside *you?* Maybe He has given you an idea, one unique, great idea for a product or service that could be worth a lot of money. Perhaps His plan is for you to start your own business marketing your idea. It doesn't matter where you are *now.* What matters is where you go from here in pursuing that which God has placed in your heart. Look deep within yourself. God has given you a dream; what will you do with it?

Maybe you are neck-deep in problems and can't see your way out. Maybe you are thinking, "That's all fine and good, but right now I can barely pay my rent and keep food on the table. How can I possibly pursue my dream? Nothing worthwhile ever comes without struggle or challenge. Remember...no pain, no gain. The secret to success is attitude. You can look at your struggles and challenges either as stumbling blocks that hold you back or as milestones on the road to success. The very fact that you are going through a problem means that God already has the answer. Nothing takes Him by surprise. You did not stumble upon a new problem and leave God scrambling for a solution. He already had the solution—from before the foundation of the world.

No matter what your situation, the important thing is to begin *now*, right where you are with whatever you have. Start moving toward your dream. If God has given you a dream, He has also given you the ability to make it a reality. Be patient. Success takes time. Someone once said, "I worked all my life to become an overnight success."

Becoming fruitful is a growth process. Apples do not suddenly pop into existence fully ripe and mature; they grow and develop over time. If we cry out to God for a tree, He may give us a seed because He wants us to grow the tree. Most of us would rather God simply give us what we ask in the way we ask for it: fully grown and developed. However, God is interested not just in delivering us, but in what we *become* through the *process* of growth and maturity. His concern is that we become fruitful, bearing fruit that is ripe and mature.

For some reason we want to sit back and expect God to hand everything to us with no effort on our part. Do we as parents do *everything* for our children? Of course not. We require them to do some things themselves, and more as they get older, so they can learn and grow. It is the same way with God. God is not a genie. He *could* do everything for us, but that would not help us learn how to be fruitful. Instead, He has placed seeds inside us—seeds of creativity, potential, and success—and expects us to cultivate, groom, and nurture them into ripe, useful fruit.

My mother always used to say, "Where there's a will, there's a way." The seeds in you will never sprout and grow until you have the will to make it happen. We can complain until we are 80 years old about never having any money, and we never will—until we take our seeds and start to groom them. God has something for each of us to do in and for His Kingdom, but some of us are so mired in financial bondage that we can't do anything. Financial bondage—or any other kind of bondage—keeps us from being fruitful. Where there's a will, there's a way. God has the way if we have the will. He created us to be fruitful and has given us the ability to produce wealth.

Drug dealers rake in millions of dollars while churches postpone or cancel needed ministries because they don't have the money. Pornographers own fancy estates around the world while many Christian believers struggle to pay their rent each month. People who give no thought at all to God drive fancy luxury cars while many of us who follow Christ seem blissfully happy driving an old 1984 Datsun held together by "I love Jesus" bumper stickers and with a soda can for a muffler. What's wrong with this picture?

We're not advocating a "name it and claim it" faith or a wealth and prosperity Gospel, but we are saying that something is wrong when so many of God's people—children of the King—are "begging bread." Somehow we have been deceived into thinking that now that we are Christians, we are not supposed to have anything. Let us ask you this: If we Christians have nothing, who will finance the end-time revival? Who will build bigger buildings and fund greater ministries? Who will buy more buses to reach more people? Who will pay for the Church's commission to take the Gospel of Christ to the nations? We've got news for you: The people in the world won't. If we, the children of God, don't do it, no one will. God put the seeds of success and greatness inside each one of us. He gave us the ability to produce wealth, and He expects us to be fruitful. Furthermore, He expects us to use our fruitfulness to advance His Kingdom and purpose in the earth.

Multiply

The second command God gave Adam and Eve was to "multiply" ("increase in number" in NIV). Notice that the command is to multiply, not add. Multiplication is a key principle in finances as well as in life. All living things, by definition, multiply, or reproduce. If they don't, they die. The same is true when it comes to money. Financial resources that do not grow and multiply eventually wither away and disappear.

We believe that with this command God is saying to us, "I have given you the power to produce wealth, so do it. Take your seed and multiply." Someone might ask, "But how *do* I multiply?" One thing is certain: You will never multiply your money as long as you hold it by yourself. It takes at least two to multiply; one cannot multiply alone. That is why God's command was to Adam and Eve *together*. Only together could they multiply.

Multiplication in the financial realm has to do with investment and return. If you want to multiply your finances, invest in something that will bring a return. Get someone else involved. Give, don't hoard. What do you do with your paycheck? If you are like most Americans, you spend it. The average American today has less than a thousand dollars in savings. What do you have to show for the money you spent? A new boat? A new car? A new set of golf clubs?

Please understand what we're saying here. There is nothing wrong with having any of those things as long as we understand that they do not multiply. Investing and giving are not the same as spending. Wise investing brings a return and an increase on the original investment; in other words—multiplication. Giving is a biblical principle that also promises a multiplied return: "Give, and it will be given to you. A good measure, pressed down, shaken together and running over, will be poured into your lap. For with the measure you use, it will be measured to you" (Luke 6:38). "Cast your bread upon the waters, for after many days you will find it again" (Ecclesiastes 11:1). Be adventurous. You can't multiply if you always try to play it safe. Remember the old proverb, "Nothing ventured, nothing gained." Don't expect to reap the benefits unless you are willing to take a few risks.

Spending, on the other hand, does not multiply. Once you have spent your money, it is gone and you get nothing more from it. All you have to show for your money is what you bought with it, which usually begins decreasing in value the moment you bring it home.

One of the problems so many of us have with our finances is that we do too much spending and not enough investing and giving. As long as we spend more than we invest or give, we will never be able to multiply our resources to the extent God desires. Too much spending eats away our assets and leaves us nothing in return. When Jesus said, "But store up for yourselves treasures in heaven, where moth and rust do not destroy, and where thieves do not break in and steal" (Matthew 6:20), He was talking about investing and giving toward things of lasting value, things that will yield an eternal return.

We have seen this principle of multiplication at work in the church where Ken is our pastor. When Ken first came as pastor, the church was focused on its own personal needs. We struggled to find the money to do such things as repair the air conditioning, put a new roof on the building, keep the yard cut, and cover over a pothole in the parking lot that looked as big as the Grand Canyon. We were simply maintaining, trying to take care of "number one." Money can't multiply like that.

That first year it seemed we would receive less than $175,000.00 in tithes and offerings. In the end, however, we actually received $195,000. Today we can receive that in one month. What made the difference? We started multiplying our money by investing and giving. Specifically, we started giving more to missions than we had ever given before. In one recent year, the children in our church alone gave over $8,000 just by bringing in change from week to week. We bought some buses so we could go out and bring people in. We began giving to other ministries, including some outside the four walls of our own church. We started to invest our resources in Kingdom work because we learned the lesson that one cannot multiply, but two can.

We even assist another church in our community by paying one of the staff salaries. Many people in that church were saved because our church invested heavily in that ministry. One cannot multiply, but two can. We will continue to do it. We will continue to move forward. Some people have said to Ken, "Pastor, you know we're trying to build this building. Why don't you lighten up on what you give to other ministries?" The answer: because of the principle of multiplication. It is a matter of seedtime and harvest. If we want an abundant harvest, we must plant seeds in somebody else's soil.

The Bible teaches that when we give, we get in return, and what we get in return is more than what we gave. We do not believe we should give *in order* to get—that is a wrong motivation. When we give from the generosity of our hearts and with faith in God's promises, He blesses us with abundant returns in accord with our giving. When our church had a need, we gave. We gave to a missionary before we fixed our air conditioner. We gave to another ministry before we fixed our parking lot. We continued to give to other ministries before and during the process of building our new building.

Look at your resources. If what you have in your hand is not big enough to be your harvest, chances are it is your seed. If you need a harvest, put your seed in the ground and grow it. Invest it in something that the Lord can multiply. So many of us live only for today, and that is why we are so deep in debt. We throw money away as if there is no tomorrow. Which is better, to take your handful of corn and hastily throw it on a gravel road where it is quickly consumed, or to plant it (invest it) in rich soil where it will sprout, grow, and multiply into an abundant harvest? You don't even have to be a farmer to figure that one out!

So many of us are taking what God has given us and throwing it on the gravel. We wonder why we can't seem to produce or get ahead even though we pay our tithes. Part of the reason is that with the other ninety percent we throw good money after bad. The Good Samaritan invested wisely in a man who needed his help. What if, however, the man he helped began to depend on the Samaritan for assistance on a daily basis, making no effort of his own to improve his situation? Pretty soon, even the benevolent Samaritan would need to find another investment for his resources—an investment that would produce.

At some point, we must learn to stop throwing our money away aimlessly. One of our biggest traps in this area is credit card interest. Many of us balk at the idea of paying ten percent to God as a tithe—"I can't afford that!"—but we gladly pay the credit card companies eighteen percent, twenty percent, or more in interest. That's corn on the gravel. Instead of paying interest to a secular bank or credit card company, wouldn't you rather invest in fertile soil that promises an abundant return? God called us to multiply, but many of us cannot because we are in financial bondage.

Replenish

God's third command to Adam and Eve was "replenish the earth" ("fill the earth" in NIV). The word *replenish* means, "to fill with persons or animals," "to fill with inspiration or power," and "to fill or build up again." This command seems to carry both the idea of filling the earth initially as well as *refilling* it continually. To "fill up again" presupposes an emptying out. When you drink a glass of water and then refill the glass, you *replenish* the water in your glass.

Here's a spiritual application first that will make the financial application easier to understand. As a pastor, I (Ken) carry a continuing burden for the spiritual welfare of my congregation. All conscientious pastors do. When I stand up to preach on Sunday, if I have done my work right, I step into the pulpit full of spiritual "water" from my study and preparation and personal time with the Lord. By the end of the service, I am empty, drained, because I have poured it all out. Before the next service I need to replenish my well. I need to get back into the presence of God, crack my Bible open, and get on my face again before the Lord so that He can begin to pour into me again.

We all need periodic times of refreshing and replenishing from the well of God's living water. Second Corinthians 4:7 says that we are "earthen vessels" ("jars of clay" in NIV) who carry inside us the treasure of the presence and glory of the Lord. The fact of the matter is, none of us are perfect vessels; we all "leak" to one degree or another. Our "jars" are cracked (some more than others!). That is why we need to replenish our water supply every so often. None of us can give and give and give without ever replenishing ourselves from the source—we'll run dry.

If water cannot move, it eventually becomes stagnant, stinking, and full of nasty things. That's why a swamp is so slimy and smells so bad. A swamp is nothing more than a river with the ends blocked up so that the water can't move anywhere. In the Middle East, the Dead Sea is dead because the water has no outlet. Water flows in constantly from the Jordan River, but it has no way out except through evaporation. Stagnation has made the alkali content of the water so high that nothing can live in it.

The same thing can happen when it comes to our finances. If we are going to be replenished, that means we must first be emptied out. In order to receive, we must give. That is where our tithe comes in. Remember that one cannot multiply; it takes two. Tithing is one way of getting God involved with our money so it can multiply. As we are faithful to give out, He is faithful to replenish. That is a proven biblical principle.

Note too, however, that God's command is for *us* to "replenish" or "fill" the earth. In financial terms this means learning to recognize that *none* of our money is our own but belongs to God, and we are responsible to Him for using the money He has entrusted us with it to serve His purposes in the world. As we use God's money for God's purposes—as we invest in His Kingdom work—we will "replenish" the earth and "fill" the world with the knowledge and the glory of God.

Like the commands to be fruitful and to multiply, the command to replenish is tied to the principle of seedtime and harvest. God's intention for us as individual believers and collectively in our churches is to invest our financial resources to help transform a lost and dying world. The problem is that too many of us have gotten trapped by the world's money system. Instead of controlling our money—what little of it we have—our money controls us. Because we are so in bondage financially, the money that we otherwise could use for God's Kingdom is controlled by people in the world, who use it for all sorts of worldly and ungodly purposes.

Subdue and Have Dominion

We want to cover the last two commands together because they are so closely related. God told Adam and Eve to "subdue" the earth and to "have dominion over" ("rule over" in NIV) every living creature on the earth. *Subdue* means, "to conquer," while *dominion* means, "to exercise control over." When God said to "subdue" the earth, He was telling them to conquer it and bring it under subjection. Once they had conquered, they were to rule and exercise control over the created order as God's designated representatives.

God created us to be conquerors. In fact, Romans 8:37 says that we are "more than conquerors through him who loved us." So many of us, however, do not live as more than conquerors when it comes to the financial matters of our lives. Jesus did not give us power to overcome in one area but leave us weak and helpless in another. He came to demolish *all* strongholds and destroy *all* the work of the enemy. Yet, in spite of this, the issue of finances remains an overpowering stronghold for many Christians.

Why is this so? Due to immaturity, irresponsibility, lack of discipline, or faulty teaching, we have allowed ourselves to come under the dominion of that which we should have dominion over. Money controls us rather than the other way around. Caught up in the consumer culture with its easy credit and buy-now-pay-later enticements, we get carried away by the promises of "instant credit" and "no interest for two years." Buying into that deception, all we ask is, "How much is the monthly payment?" Because of our hunger for instant gratification, we give no thought to the interest rate we're paying or how long it will take to pay for what we buy. Some of the things we buy on credit stop working or wear out years before we finish paying for them. That is like throwing our corn on the gravel.

In many ways, consumer "credit" is a myth. Credit card companies send us their credit cards and tell us we now have "credit." That is somewhat misleading. As soon as we use the card, our "credit" becomes *debt*. Debt is a form of bondage because it places us and our money under the control of someone else—specifically, a credit card company, a bank, or some other lending institution. Every financial decision we make has to take into account the money we owe to cover our indebtedness. The "freedom" of buying on credit is deceptive; in reality it could lead to the bondage of debt.

God said that we are to subdue and have dominion—to conquer and control. We will never have power over anything that we do not control. As long as we are in debt we will never truly control our money. Neither will we know financial freedom. Proverbs 22:7 says, "The rich rule over the poor, and the borrower is servant to the lender." The Hebrew word for *servant* in this verse literally means, "bondservant," which refers to a much deeper level of servitude than does the word *servant*. An equivalent word would be "slave."

When it comes to money, many of us have a problem controlling our spending. There is another word for a problem we cannot control: *addiction*. Too many of us are addicted to spending, and the credit card companies and lending institutions stand ever ready to help us feed our habit. The more we spend, the more credit they extend (as long as we make regular payments) until they have us strung out with a balance of debt that will take years to pay off at the minimum monthly payment.

Like any addiction, an addiction to spending takes valuable resources away from other, more important and needful things in life. If all your resources are tied up in paying your debts, what will you do when emergencies come? What if the water main bursts or the car breaks down or you lose your job? What if a great opportunity for ministry comes up—an overseas mission trip, for example—and you have to pass because you lack the free financial resources to go?

Unless we control our money, our money will control us. God created us to prosper—to be fruitful, multiply, replenish, subdue, and have dominion. We should be the lenders, not the borrowers; the head and not the tail. Our ability both to receive blessings from God and be a blessing to others depends largely on how well we control and manage all our resources, and that includes our finances. In every area of life, the more faithful we are with what we have, the more the Lord will entrust to us.

We will never be blessed financially until we learn to conquer and control our money. Somehow we must break the chains of bad teaching, bad choices, and bad habits that hold us in financial bondage. As with any addiction, the first step toward recovery for many of us will be to recognize the symptoms of bondage and acknowledge that we have a problem. The next chapter will help us better understand financial bondage: what it is, how we get there, and how to identify its symptoms.

CHAPTER THREE

THE TRAP OF FINANCIAL BONDAGE

Like it or not, money is a spiritual issue. Many people, even in Christian circles, are in bondage to things related to money and don't even realize it. Where financial matters are concerned, bondage occurs on two sides: the poverty side and the prosperity side. On the poverty side, one visit to a third world country or to the inner city of one of America's major metropolises is all it takes to understand the binding and devastating effects of poverty. Poverty itself is a spiritual issue, a curse that needs to be broken, perpetuated by ignorance, lack of opportunity, a "poverty mindset" that expects nothing better, and sometimes, even prejudice.

On the other hand, prosperity can carry its own kind of bondage. We can own so much stuff that our stuff owns us. No matter how much we have, it is never enough. Nothing satisfies us. Wrongly believing that happiness and contentment lie in how much we have, we consume our days always trying to get more.

Materialism has nothing to do with how much we make. We have seen people who make $30,000 a year who are more materialistic than people who make $100,000 a year. Poor people and rich people alike can be obsessed with money: the poor with *getting* money and the rich with getting *more* money.

The issue with money is not *amount* but *attitude*. God wants to bless us financially and has given us the ability to produce wealth (see Deuteronomy 8:18). Too often, however, we short-circuit that wealth-making ability in our lives by our own improper attitude and practices where money is concerned. Statistics show that Christians are in just as much debt as non-Christians. We may have all sorts of great financial dreams and plans, only to discover when the opportunity comes that our bondage to debt keeps us from acting on them. Our chance for freedom passes us by and we are left in chains, slaves to our poor financial decisions.

Israel—From Bondage to Freedom

Being in financial bondage can be compared to the plight of the children of Israel in Egypt. For over four hundred years they were literally slaves of the Egyptians. They had very little they could call their own. Their time was not their own. Their labor was not their own. They had no freedom, no rights, and no prospects. Every aspect of their lives was controlled by the whim and will of Pharaoh.

When God got ready to take them out of Egypt under Moses' leadership, He saw to it that they did not leave empty-handed. God gave the Israelites favor in the eyes of their Egyptian neighbors, who showered them with all kinds of gold and silver objects, jewelry, and other precious treasures. The Israelites walked out carrying the wealth of Egypt, and they didn't even have to fight for it. Guided by God's sure hand, the children of Israel walked out of their dark night of bondage and poverty into their new dawn of freedom and plenty.

Many Christians and churches today are stumbling around in their own dark night. In the ten years from 1986 to 1996 alone, approximately 100,000 churches in our country closed their doors, many for financial reasons. Many more have closed in the years since. Some people today are pronouncing that the day of the Church is dead, that our nation has entered a post-Christian era, and that we can no longer call ourselves a Christian nation. It appears as though the Church by and large is like Israel in Egypt—caught in bondage and poverty. We seem to be in a bad position.

It was the same way with the Israelites. Even after Moses appeared on the scene, things got worse before they got better. After Moses' first attempt to free the people, Pharaoh turned up the heat. He required the Israelites to continue producing the same quota of bricks, but no longer provided the straw. They had to collect it themselves. A battle of wills ensued—the will of Pharaoh against the will of God. Ten plagues later, with Egypt whipped and "on the ropes," the Israelites walked to freedom heavy laden with Egyptian treasures and in full health. The Bible says that there was not a sick person among them.

We believe that we are living in a similar time. The devil is at work and the "pharaohs" of our world are turning up the heat against the church. A new day, a new era, is about to dawn. The time is near when God is going to say to His people, "Go get what belongs to you. Grab your stuff. Take back what the enemy took from you and put it back where it belongs." When our Lord Jesus Christ returns for His Bride, His Church, we will not leave here in bondage. We will not leave in sickness or in poverty. When we leave, we will leave triumphantly, heavy laden with all the stuff that the devil at one time stole from us. Like the nation of Israel, the destiny of the Church is freedom, not bondage, and prosperity, not poverty.

This freedom and prosperity are not just spiritual, but financial as well. We believe that as the return of Christ nears, there will be a revival of financial stability and prosperity in churches and in Christian homes. The only way this will happen, however, is for us to begin to understand the principles and precepts in the Word of God concerning the subject of finances. If there is going to be a great last days outpouring of God's Spirit resulting in many, many people being saved, we are going to need more "barns" in which to store the harvest. We *must* have a revival in our finances. As long as we Christians are in bondage to debt, we will not be able to do much. How can we finance the work of the Kingdom of God if all our money is tied up in paying for the things of the world? That is why we insist that the subject of finances is a spiritual issue.

The children of Israel left Egypt heavy laden with gold, silver, and other treasures. There is no biblical reason why God's people should fear, shun, or reject money. Although reaching lost souls for Christ should always be our first priority, we should also take great care to present to the community a church facility that is clean, in good repair, and looks good. After all, we are a reflection of our Father, the King.

God is extravagant. As the Creator and owner of all there is, He can afford to be. Some biblical scholars estimate that the tabernacle the Israelites built in the wilderness at God's direction was worth 87 billion dollars by today's standards! That's extravagant! God is so extravagant that He paved the streets of Heaven with gold and made its gates out of pearl.

Not an Amount but an Attitude

When it comes to money, the important thing is not the *amount* of our money, but our *attitude* toward our money. One of the first things we must learn in this regard is that with money, as with everything else, we are managers, not owners. Understanding this truth alone will make an enormous difference in the approach we take to our finances. God is the owner of all things. Those things which we call our own, whether money or possessions, in truth belong to God. He has simply entrusted them to our care and management. How much more He entrusts to us depends on how good a job we do in managing what He has already given us.

Whether we control our money or our money controls us, whether we possess things or are possessed by them, depends on our attitude. Our attitude will reveal who we are truly serving. Jesus made this very clear when He said:

> *"Whoever can be trusted with very little can also be trusted with much, and whoever is dishonest with very little will also be dishonest with much. So if you have not been trustworthy in handling worldly wealth, who will trust you with true riches? And if you have not been trustworthy with someone else's property, who will give you property of your own? No servant can serve two masters. Either he will hate the one and love the other, or he will be devoted to the one and despise the other. You cannot serve both God and Money."*   Luke 16:10-13

Before we can be trusted with much, we must prove ourselves trustworthy with a little. Little or much makes no difference because it is attitude, not amount, that counts. Are you so steeped in debt that you have no financial flexibility? Does your captivity to spending prevent you from giving, investing, and saving? Do you struggle day by day just to get by financially and wonder why you can't get ahead no matter how hard you try? Maybe you are not being trustworthy in managing what God has already given you. Maybe you do not have more because God cannot yet trust you with more. Learn to wisely manage the little you have and God will give you more.

"Whoever can be trusted with very little can also be trusted with much." It all boils down to attitude. Someone came up to Ken once and said, "I would give if I won the lottery." His response was, "You need to learn how to give *now*." Maybe you are saying, "I can't afford to give to God." The truth is, you can't afford *not* to give to God. You will never get unless you start to give. That is an undeniable spiritual principle.

Verse 11 says, "If you have not been trustworthy in handling worldly wealth, who will trust you with true riches?" We will never have true wealth if we are not first faithful with money. There is a big difference between money and wealth. Money has to do with *amount*, while wealth is an *attitude*. Not all wealthy people have a lot of money, but they do understand what is truly important in life and apply their resources to those things. We both know people who grew up in poverty who thought they were rich because their parents were good stewards and paid attention to first things first.

If we are not faithful with our money, God will never trust us with real riches. There is nothing wrong with having a lot of money or with being wealthy as long as we know what to do with our wealth. Someone has to finance what God wants to do in these last days. God will entrust His riches to those who prove faithful and trustworthy in using those riches in accordance with His will.

Contrary to what many people believe, more money does not solve problems. If our attitude about money is wrong, having more of it will only magnify the problems we already have, as well as create new ones. Jesus told the story of a rich man whose land produced such an abundant crop that he had nowhere to store all his harvest. His solution was to build bigger barns to hold his crop so he could "take life easy, eat, drink and be merry" (Luke 12:19). All his efforts were in vain, however, because that very night the man died and found himself standing before God.

This rich man had the wrong attitude about money and wealth, seeking only comfort, ease, and pleasure for himself. His obsession with the riches of the world left him poor in the things of God so that when his soul was required of him, he was not ready. If our pursuit of wealth is out of a desire to be free of problems and worry, we have the wrong attitude. Our focus is in the wrong place. More money and material wealth will not free us of problems in life. It's not an *amount* but an *attitude*. It's not what we *have* that counts but what we *do* with what we have. I read about a man who went from making $45,000 one year to $175,000 the following year. At the end of both years he had zero in savings. It's not an *amount* but an *attitude*.

Our attitude toward money will be reflected in the things we give priority to in life. We claim to be born-again Christians who love the Lord and have given our lives to Him. Does our day planner reflect that claim? How about our checkbook? We all spend our time and money on that which is most important to us. Where are your priorities? How much time and money do you spend on your own hobbies, interests, and pleasures? How much time and money do you invest in the things of the Lord and the work of His Kingdom?

We are not saying that hobbies and personal interests are wrong, but we do believe that if we invest more in them than we do in the Lord's work, we need to reevaluate our priorities. One man we both know loves to spend a lot of money taking other guys out golfing. When there is a need in the church, however, this same man will gladly give a hundred times more to that need than he spent on the golfing outing. It's not a matter of spending money on personal interests and fun activities. The issue is where our priorities are in life. It's not an *amount* but an *attitude*.

The Subtlety of Debt

Unfortunately for many of us, our financial priorities are revealed every month when we open our credit card and loan statements. Because of many ill-considered prior decisions, *repayment of debt* is our biggest financial priority. Debt is a subtle trap, very easy to fall into but extremely difficult to climb out of.

Not long ago a man said to Ken, "You know, Pastor, I don't really want to be rich. I don't have a desire for a whole lot of wealth. I just wish that every time I opened my wallet I would find another dollar bill in there, that every time I spent money I would still have money left."

That is exactly the philosophy of many Americans. We always want more. There is always something else to buy, something new that catches our eye. Our spending is limited only by our imagination. If that runs out, there are always television commercials and other advertisements to give us new ideas of ways to spend our money.

Financial management is a spiritual issue. For this reason we need to recognize and be alert to the tricks of the devil. He seeks to deceive and entrap us in this area just as he does everywhere else. The devil is very subtle; he will not attack us with the obvious. The Bible says that Satan is cunning and crafty. He will sneak in unawares, try to catch us off guard, and slip his shackles on us before we know what is happening. I believe that one of Satan's primary targets is the financial affairs of the American people, and especially of Christians. Like the serpent he is, he has slithered his way into our lives and oh, so subtly put his clamps on us. One of his most effective weapons is the allure of the debt trap.

There once was a story about a family from over a century ago that wanted to move out west during one of the big gold strikes. Many of their friends and neighbors were pulling up stakes and heading out to take advantage of the new opportunity. This one particular family wanted to join the others but could not move because they had debt on their farm. It was a debt of only five dollars, but it was still more than they could pay. Their debt tied them to their farm so that they could not move when a better opportunity arose. In addition, people in the community looked down on this family because they owed money. In those days, debt was seen as a curse and certainly as a disgrace.

We certainly live in a different world today. In our society today debt is seen not as a curse or disgrace but as the normal state of affairs. Our entire credit-driven economy is built on the expectation that people will enter into debt. All the credit card companies depend for their existence on the fact that the majority of card-holders will pay off their debts in monthly installments plus interest. It is a system that most of us take for granted.

Credit is fine as long as we can control it. This means being able to pay it in full each month. Instead, most of us adopt a "play now, pay later" philosophy where we choose instant gratification and give little thought to the long-term effects of installment payments with compounded interest. That is just one of the subtle ways the enemy lures us into financial bondage. Notice that we said Satan *lures* us. We cannot blame the devil for our financial bondage when it is we who made the choices that put us there. Satan places the temptation before us; he lays out the enticing options in front of our eyes, but we make the choices and therefore bear the full responsibility for the consequences of those choices.

Compared to the rest of the world, America is a very rich and affluent nation. Our affluence can be a blessing but can just as easily be a curse if we don't know how to handle it. It is so easy in America to get into debt. There is even a popular notion that says you can *borrow* money to get out of debt! It is called a *consolidation loan*. How logical is that? The only value of a consolidation loan is that by getting several debts combined into one lower monthly payment you reduce your monthly outgo and may save some interest. A consolidation loan is still a loan and therefore still a debt. It may take longer to pay off than any of the original debts would have.

As of 1996, Americans possessed nearly four hundred and fifty million credit cards. In that same year, 2.7 billion solicitations for new credit cards were mailed out, an average of seventeen credit cards for every adult. That is a recipe for bondage. Proverbs 22:7 says, "The rich rule over the poor, and the borrower is servant to the lender." We see the truth of this verse borne out in America every day. The people with the money make the decisions and the people without money have little choice but to follow along. People in debt have made themselves "servants" of those to whom they owe money. They are bound by the rules set by the lender, which rarely if ever favor the borrower.

America today is a nation of debtors. In our constant craving for instant gratification and for "getting ahead" we have become slaves to those who lend money. They become our "master" so to speak, dictating to us when and how much to pay. This, in turn, dictates what we do and affects the choices we make. Because of our debt, our financial choices are very limited. Rather than financing our children's college education or financing the work of the church and of God's Kingdom, we spend all our time and energy financing our debt. We are chained to a ravenous monster that relentlessly consumes our assets and leaves nothing in return.

Owe No Man Anything

Don't misunderstand us. No one should feel condemned just because they have debt. Most of us are in debt of some kind to one degree or another. Debt is not necessarily evil in and of itself. It depends on our attitude toward it and how we deal with it. Many of us have heard Romans 13:8 applied to this issue of indebtedness: "Owe no man any thing, but to love one another: for he that loveth another hath fulfilled the law" (KJV). This verse has often been misquoted and misapplied to condemn indebtedness of any kind. That's not really what Paul is saying. The NIV translation of the verse captures more of the meaning: "Let no debt remain outstanding, except the continuing debt to love one another, for he who loves his fellowman has fulfilled the law."

Paul is not saying necessarily that we should never borrow, but that when we do borrow we should pay back what we have borrowed. In practical terms this means that if a friend borrowed ten dollars from you yesterday for lunch, he needs to pay you back. It is a simple matter of honesty, character, and integrity. Failure to repay what we owe is wrong, as Psalm 37:21 makes clear: "The wicked borrow and do not repay, but the righteous give generously." Whenever we borrow, we have a God-given responsibility to repay, and He will hold us accountable. Sometimes that accountability will take the form of continuing financial hardship no matter what we do. In effect, God curses our finances until we get ourselves right.

The second part of the verse speaks to another godly financial principle. Every time that God deals with the subject of finances in the Christian life, or the God-believing life, He talks about giving generously. Never once does He tell us to hoard our goods. Never once does He advise us to stockpile our resources. The closest He comes is when Jesus tells us to lay up for ourselves treasures in Heaven. In Jesus' parable from Luke chapter 12, the rich man received rebuke and judgment from God for his desire to store up his abundance for himself by building bigger barns.

It's very interesting that in Psalm 37:21, David, who composed the psalm, identifies debt as a moral issue rather than a financial issue. Failure to repay a debt is an act of wickedness and is therefore a reflection of character because wickedness is a condition of the heart. It all comes down to attitude again. To use someone else's money and not return it, or to become delinquent in payment, or to default on a debt is nothing less than stealing. The eighth commandment says, "Thou shalt not steal" (Exodus 20:15, KJV). We violate that commandment every time we borrow or use something that belongs to some-body else and do not return it, or in the case of money, repay it.

Statistics show that Christians borrow just as much as non-Chris-tians and have similar records of delinquency in payment. We're not talking about emergencies or contingencies that come up such as se-rious illness or job loss. No. We're talking about people—Christians—who simply flat out do not pay. In their attitude and mind they have said, "Forget it." That is not a godly example to set before an ungodly world. As Christians we are called to the highest standard of honesty, integrity, and moral uprightness. Trustworthiness in repaying legiti-mate financial obligations should be an absolute *minimum* for us. What message do we send to the world when we as Christians play fast and loose with our financial responsibilities?

Whenever we borrow, we enter into an agreement, whether spo-ken or written, to pay it back. We give our word to repay the debt in full. Failure to do so is to go back on our word, making us liars and guilty of thievery. As Romans 13:8 indicates, we have a biblical and moral obligation to leave no debt unpaid. To adopt any other attitude or practice is to shut ourselves off from the financial blessings God wants to give us.

The "Can't Wait" Trap

Debt can lure us in through many different avenues. Let's talk about three "debt traps" to watch out for that are particularly enticing: the "can't wait" trap, the comparison trap, and the commodation trap.

The "can't wait" trap is the trap of instant gratification, the "I can't wait; I've got to have it now!" syndrome. We're so used to drive-through windows, "buy now, pay later" offers, and five-minute microwave meals that we have forgotten how to be patient. Many of us today, particularly the younger generation, know next to nothing about the concept of delayed reward. Everything has to be now, now, now, to-day, today, today. We heard of one store where you can go in, order a meal, and go shopping while it is being prepared. When your meal is ready, it is brought out to you so that you can eat while you shop. Talk about instant gratification! Nobody likes to wait for anything anymore. We are all in such a hurry; we buy things left and right as if there will be no tomorrow. As far as our attitude and spending habits are con-cerned, patience is no longer a virtue.

Adding to the problem is the fact that we have so many choices; so many products are available. By the year 1987 there were more shopping centers in America than schools. The average supermarket stocks over 30,000 different items. What parent of small children today does not dread going down the cereal aisle? Over 11,000 magazines are published in America.

The credit card companies don't help. We have to constantly be on our guard. Even when you go shopping with cash, there will always be someone in a store somewhere offering an extra discount if you will use your credit card or, even better, *sign up* for a credit card. They know just how to play on our "can't wait" mentality. Do you pay for Christmas gifts with a credit card? That's like pouring money down a hole in the ground. Statistics show that most Americans are still paying off last year's Christmas gifts on their credit card when next Christmas comes. How tragic. How silly and senseless! Think about it: one, two, three, four, or more years later still paying for something that didn't last a year or that you ended up selling at the July 4th garage sale! It would be funny if it wasn't so sad.

Today we can even shop by the Internet. We don't need a car, a store, or even cash money. All we need is a computer and a credit card and we can spend millions. Internet shopping is now a multibillion-dollar-a-year industry and shows no signs of slowing.

There was a time when patience was considered a virtue. In our present buying climate, patience has become a vice. After all, why wait if we can have what we want when we want it and delivered right to our front door? Somehow as Christians we have got to get back to the spiritual fruit of patience and self-control. Our modern society does not encourage either. In our consumer culture, every move, every strategy by a merchant is designed to entice us to spend that next dollar, not tomorrow or next week or next year, but today—right now. It is the "can't wait" trap, and all of us have fallen into it at one time or another.

There are a lot of people in debt who need "plastic surgery." They need to take a pair of scissors to their credit cards and be done with it. Don't get me wrong; we're not saying that it is wrong necessarily to have a credit card or to be in debt. Light or moderate debt under control is okay, particularly if our goal is to get it paid off as soon as possible. Sometimes circumstances make going into debt necessary. As far as credit cards are concerned, they are often necessary today in order to do any traveling: renting a car, making hotel and airline reservations, etc. The key is careful planning. Using credit or going into debt with no plan for getting out is a recipe for trouble.

The big danger of a credit card is that it is so easy to whip it out and use it without thinking about it. Most people who are in trouble over debt got that way through impulsive spending—buying on a whim. We need to think before we spend. We heard of one couple who avoided the "can't wait" trap by using what they called "frozen assets." They put their credit card in a bowl of water and stuck it in the freezer. Every time they thought they wanted to go out and purchase something, they had to get that bowl out of the freezer and let the ice melt. By the time they could get to their credit card, they had had enough time to think through whether or not they really needed the item they wanted to buy. That's a good strategy. Anything we can do that will buy us time to think before we act will help us avoid the "can't wait" trap with its impulsive spending.

The Comparison Trap

A second dangerous debt trap is the comparison trap; a trap that many of us insist does not affect us. We need to be honest with ourselves and reconsider. The comparison trap is the trap of peer pressure: Everybody else has it so we have to have it also. None of us are automatically immune to this trap. Avoiding it requires careful attention and diligence.

Studies show that the buying patterns of those around us determine what we buy. Let's face it: We want what our neighbors have and what our coworkers have. If we do not have what they have, we feel somehow as though we are missing out on something or that there is something wrong with us. Unless we have what everybody else has, we feel incomplete or inadequate. It doesn't matter whether they make more money than we do or whether we can afford it; what matters is "keeping up with the Joneses."

In America, keeping up with the Joneses has become a national pastime. Thanks to television and the other mass media, it has become much bigger than staying on a par with the next-door neighbors. Now we can watch the lifestyles of the rich and famous. Television and Hollywood celebrities are shown with their expensive clothes, luxury cars, mansion estates, and private jets. Madison Avenue barrages us with ads for all sorts of things that we simply "can't live without," whether or not we can afford them. That's when society tells us that our credit card can be the great "equalizer." As long as there is room on the credit line, we can emulate almost anything we want to.

How can we avoid the comparison trap? A good place to start is to remember the ninth commandment: "You shall not covet your neighbor's house. You shall not covet your neighbor's wife, or his manservant or maidservant, his ox or donkey, or anything that belongs to your neighbor" (Exodus 20:17). God has commanded us not to covet— not to crave for ourselves what other people have. Once again, it comes down to our attitude. As long as we see "things" as the goal of life, we will never escape the comparison trap. Once we realize that there is much more to life than the acquisition of possessions, possessions will cease to have a tight grip on our hearts. Jesus said, "Watch out! Be on your guard against all kinds of greed; a man's life does not consist in the abundance of his possessions" (Luke 12:15). He followed this warning with His parable we looked at earlier about the rich man who built bigger barns to store his harvest.

God does not give commandments in order to deprive us of any good thing. His commandments are in our own best interest because He loves us and knows what we really need. The commandment against coveting is designed to protect us against the sin and corruption of greed. There is nothing wrong with looking at someone who has been blessed and be inspired to move up, improve, and do better things ourselves. At the same time, we must be careful, because there is a very thin line between being inspired by someone's prosperity and coveting it. God gave us the commandment against coveting because He knows that coveting will suck us into the comparison trap, leading to the bondage of debt.

The "Commodation" Trap

The third debt trap, the "commodation" trap, is probably the must subtle and dangerous of the three because it plays to our ego. Once we learn to recognize this trap for what it is, we will begin to see advertisements in a different way. Here is how the "commodation" trap works. We see or hear advertisements that say, "Huge savings! Huge savings on everything in the store!" Then they try to sell you on accommodating you and making your life comfortable. "If you don't deserve it, who does? Now you can afford to be good to yourself. You can't afford to miss this sale!" Now, there's a paradoxical statement if I've ever heard one! "You can't afford to miss this sale!" In other words, you can't afford *not* to buy this. That's just plain crazy!

Advertising uses enticements like, "Be good to yourself. You deserve it. You work hard for your money. You've earned it. Come on out and enjoy a nice…" whatever the product is. The "commodation" trap plays on our attitude even more than the other two traps because it works to convince us that we are *entitled* to all these things and that not to have them is an unfair deprivation. In other words, this trap feeds our selfishness by causing us to feel unsatisfied with what we have and to crave more.

We have already talked about the importance of learning to be content with what we have. Attitude is everything. King Solomon had a lot to say about the futility of always wanting more:

> *Whoever loves money never has money enough; whoever loves wealth is never satisfied with his income. This too is meaningless. As goods increase, so do those who consume them. And what benefit are they to the owner except to feast his eyes on them? The sleep of a laborer is sweet, whether he eats little or much, but the abundance of a rich man permits him no sleep.*
>
> Ecclesiastes 5:10-12

These words come from a man who knew what he was talking about. Solomon, a son of David, was the richest man in the world in his day. He had anything and everything he could possibly need or want. Yet he found that all of it was meaningless, because no matter how much he had, he always wanted more.

Part of our problem with these debt traps is that we are afflicted with "destination disease" and don't even know it. Destination disease is the attitude that says we will be happy once we are somewhere else or something specific has changed in our lives. "I will be happy if I can buy that house," or "I will be happy when I get that new job," or "I will be happy when I buy that new car." That is deceptive. We need to learn how to be happy *now*, not somewhere down the line. If we cannot learn to be happy now with what we have now, we will never be happy when we get what we are after, because possessions do not bring happiness. True happiness is an attitude and condition of the heart and does not depend on the level of our material abundance. If we are happy with a little, we will be happy with a lot. If we are not happy with a little, we will never be happy no matter how much we have.

Ultimately, if we are in financial bondage because of debt, we have no one to blame but ourselves. We are each responsible for our own choices. If we make unwise financial decisions, we should not be surprised at having to bear the consequences. When we experience financial difficulty, it is very easy to blame someone else rather than acknowledge our own responsibility: "If my boss would just pay me enough, I wouldn't be in this fix." Yes, you would. If you got in bondage with a little, you would get in bondage with a lot; it's not an amount but an attitude. Your boss is not responsible for your financial bondage. He is responsible to pay you what he owes you in wages, but he is not responsible for what you do with your pay. If you agree to a job making $10.00 an hour, don't get into $20.00 an hour's worth of debt and then expect your boss to bail you out with a raise. That's not his responsibility.

Years ago, when I (Ken) was just starting out in marriage and in ministry, I worked a job in construction. Money was tight because my wife and I were trying to buy a house. One day I went to my boss and said, "I need a raise." He looked at me and replied, "I don't give raises because of needs." His response made me angry, but as I studied the problem later from a biblical perspective, the Lord showed me that my boss was right.

In Matthew 20:1-16, Jesus tells a parable about a landowner who hired men to work in his fields. Early in the morning he hired a group who agreed to work all day for the sum of one denarius. At various times throughout the day he hired other workers. At the end of the day he paid all the workers one denarius, even the men who had worked only one hour. This caused the men hired in the morning to complain that they should have gotten more. They had no leg to stand on when the landowner reminded them that they had *agreed* to work for one denarius. Although the main point of this parable is the spiritual truth that God treats all who come into His Kingdom the same no matter when they come or how much they have done, the financial application is still valid. We bear responsibility for the financial decisions we make.

Each of these three debt traps—the "can't wait" trap, the comparison trap, and the "commodation" trap—have one common denominator: *self.* "*I* can't wait; *I* must have it now." "Everyone else has one, so *I* must have one, too." "*I* deserve this. *I* worked hard for it and *I* owe it to *myself*." Ken's wife used to direct a children's choir. One song they sang was called "I Trouble." It was all about "I": "I can't wait." "I deserve better." "I want to be like Susie." "I want to be like Mike." The whole song talked about the trouble that comes from focusing always on "I."

Such self-centeredness is the opposite of the life we are supposed to live as Christians. The more we live for Christ, the more we will learn to die to self. This is just as true in financial matters as in any others. Getting out of financial bondage is all about getting rid of our "I trouble." It is about dying to self, crucifying our own will and desires in favor of God's will. Getting out of financial bondage is learning to say as Jesus did, "Father, not My will but Yours be done." If we prayed that prayer every time we got ready to spend money, we would make fewer purchases. Many of us as Christians have left the Father's house with all His blessings and abundance and gone into the "far country" of selfishness and financial bondage. It is time for us to come to our senses and return so that we may be restored financially and in every other way.

CHAPTER FOUR

TOUCHING THE FORBIDDEN FRUIT

One of the foundational concepts that we need to understand before we go any further on the subject of money is that *God owns everything*. We've mentioned that before, but it bears repeating because we all have trouble truly believing it. Oh, we may give lip service to the idea that everything belongs to God, but our attitudes and actions tell a different story. Actions speak louder than words. It is what we *do* with our money and other financial resources—not what we *say*—that reveals what we really believe about God's ownership.

As a pastor, I (Ken) could not begin to count the number of times someone has asked me, "Why is it that I pay my tithe but still do not have enough? Why am I still living hand-to-mouth? Why don't I have enough money to pay my bills?" Almost without exception the answer lies not with their tithing of ten percent but with their use of the other ninety percent. Being faithful with the tithe is one thing; being faithful with the remainder is another. If God owns *everything*, then one hundred percent of what we have belongs to Him. Just because He only requires ten percent to be returned directly to Him as a tithe does not mean that we are free to do whatever we want with the rest. The other ninety percent still belongs to Him.

Although few of us would come right out and say it, our attitude toward our money often is, "Okay, I've paid God His share, and the rest is *mine*!" As long as we think and live under the mistaken notion that ninety percent belongs to us, we will never experience the kind of blessings—financial or otherwise—that God wants to give us. For example, even if you pay your tithe faithfully, how can you expect God to bless you when you use part of the remainder to buy books and magazines or rent videos with language or content that dishonors God? How can you expect God to honor you when you fail to honor Him? Let's say there is a critical ministry need in the church but you insist on spending "your" ninety percent on your own desires and pleasures, saying, "I've already given my tithe; what more do they want?" How can God bless such an attitude?

Once we truly understand that God owns everything, our whole attitude and behavior toward what we have will change. Instead of paying our tithe and then running off to do what we please, we will come back to God and ask, "What shall I do with the rest?" It is a matter of recognizing that we are not owners but *managers* and therefore responsible to God—the owner—for what we do with every penny.

Psalm 50:10 says that God owns "the cattle on a thousand hills." As the old southern preacher might say, "And He owns them thar hills too, pardner!" It's true. Look around and you will not find anything that God does not own. He created the sun, the moon, all the planets, and all the stars, and His command holds them in their orbits. Everything is His because He created it, from the farthest galaxy at the edge of space to the tiniest atoms in our bodies. He owns the air and the birds that fly in it. He owns the seas and the creatures that swim there. He owns the land and all life that lives upon it. He owns all the gold and silver and diamonds and other precious metals and gems that have ever been dug out of the earth or ever will be.

Then God created man in His own image and said, "I am giving you dominion over the earth and its resources so that you can manage them for Me." Man was created as a manager, not an owner. In the Garden of Eden, God placed reasonable restrictions on Adam and Eve's activities to reflect this owner-manager relationship. Everything went fine until the day they violated that relationship. By taking hold of the "forbidden fruit," they tried to take what was God's and make it their own. They tried to become owners.

Management Trouble in the Garden

Nowhere in the story of Adam and Eve are they presented as owners. Adam was the caretaker, or manager, of the Garden of Eden: "The LORD God took the man and put him in the Garden of Eden to work it and take care of it" (Genesis 2:15). Even though the Scriptures do not specifically state this, I am sure that Eve assisted Adam in this work after she appeared on the scene. After all, she was created to be a "helper suitable" for Adam (Genesis 2:18).

From the beginning, work was part of their daily activity, but it was not the unpleasant grind it so often became after the fall. In the beginning, caring for the Garden was a joy. No poison ivy. No dandelions. No mosquitoes. No weeds. No need for fertilizer. Just a beautiful utopia, a glorious paradise of incredible fertility and fruitfulness. God said to Adam, "You will be the lord of the Garden, and I'll be the Lord of lords. Adam, you have full dominion. You will be the king of the lion. You will be the king of the jungle. You will be the king of the Garden, and I will be the King of kings. You will be lord in the Garden, and I will be the Lord in Heaven. You will be king in the Garden and I will be King in Heaven. You have dominion here and I will have dominion there."

This account from the second chapter of Genesis reveals God's ownership in at least two ways. First, it was God who assigned Adam his role as caretaker of the Garden; Adam did not choose it for himself. Secondly, God placed a specific restriction on Adam's activity. Both of these are rightful, legitimate actions of an owner. God's restriction was very simple: "And the LORD God commanded the man, 'You are free to eat from any tree in the garden; but you must not eat from the tree of the knowledge of good and evil, for when you eat of it you will surely die'" (Genesis 2:16-17). Essentially, within that boundary, Adam was free to do as he pleased in managing his domain. Can you imagine the freedom he enjoyed?

Suppose you were invited to live in a friend's house for six months while he was overseas. Suppose your friend said, "Move your own furniture in. Paint the rooms any color you like. Decorate the house to suit your own taste. Help yourself to the vegetables from the garden. Use the barbeque grill whenever you want. Invite friends over for dinner. Throw some parties. Make it your home for the next six months." You would feel pretty free, wouldn't you?

Now suppose your friend said, "However, there is one restriction. Whatever you do, don't go into the room at the end of the hall. That is private and off limits to you. The rest of the house is yours. You have free reign; just stay out of that one room." How would you feel then?

Would you consider that a reasonable request, or an unfair restriction on your freedom? It all depends on whether you were thinking as a manager or as an owner. If you were smart, not only would you not enter the room at the end of the hall, but just to be on the safe side, you wouldn't even walk down the hall.

Adam and Eve had everything going for them: peace, joy, innocence, a beautiful environment perfectly suited for them, meaningful labor, an open relationship with their Creator, and an earthly dominion of their own. But they lost it all when they touched what God said not to touch. Eve's sin did not begin when she bit into the fruit, but when she began to look longingly at it. "That fruit sure is pretty. It looks really sweet and juicy. I wonder how it tastes." Thought leads to action, often very subtly.

Sin entices us the same way. One thought leads to another, then another, until we become obsessed with what we cannot have. A single glance down the hallway leads to a longer look, then a lingering gaze. Before long you are walking down the hallway to the door of that forbidden room. You place your hand on the doorknob and try to look through the keyhole. Curiosity and desire overcome caution and you open the door a crack. The next thing you know, you have stepped inside and violated the trust placed in you.

We do it all the time. "I know this movie has some bad stuff in it, but I'm mature. I can handle it." "That cashier gave me too much change. Oh well, they'll never miss it." "Money is really tight this month. I'll use the tithe money to pay the electric bill...just this once."

Everything was fine in the Garden until Adam and Eve forgot that they were only managers and started acting like owners. With all the abundance and freedom around them, with all the other trees at their disposal—apple, peach, pear, pomegranate, orange—they began to fixate on the one tree God had placed off limits. "Why can't we have that one too? After all, it's only one tree." That wasn't the point. The point was that they were managers, God was the owner, and He had said, "Don't go there."

From the standpoint of finances, think of the forbidden tree as symbolic of the tithe. God said, "Here is the ninety percent—this tree, that tree, those over there, and all the others. This one over here, though, is Mine. Leave this tree—this ten percent—alone." Just as God gave Adam and Eve a wonderful abundance of trees for their use, He has also given us great freedom in the use of the resources He has placed at our disposal. Our finances are not supposed to be strained or a source of continuing struggle for us. The only restriction God has placed on us is to leave the tithe alone—hold it sacred—and to manage the other ninety percent wisely and use it in ways that honor Him. Some Christians tithe faithfully but abuse the other ninety percent, while other believers bring a curse on their finances by touching the forbidden fruit—stealing God's tithe.

In spite of God's warning, Adam and Eve ate of the tree of the knowledge of good and evil. As soon as they did, the garden and everything in it became cursed. All of a sudden, apples had worms, bananas had bruises, and roses had thorns. Poison ivy sprang up. The rich ground turned hard and unyielding. Only by hard work and the sweat of their brow would they pull a harvest from the soil. "Wait! What's that commotion? I think I hear a lion growling at a lamb. *That's* never happened before! There goes the lion with lamb's blood all over its mouth! What's going on? What has happened to my garden?"

The Garden became cursed because Adam and Eve touched the one thing they shouldn't have touched. Anytime we touch what God has reserved for Himself, we bring a curse on ourselves and our situation. When the Israelites under Joshua fought against the city of Ai, they suffered a great defeat because one man, Achan, had defied the ban and taken for himself some of the spoil that God had dedicated for destruction. Achan touched the "forbidden fruit," bringing a curse down upon himself and all the Israelites. In the end, it cost Achan his life.

Eve's sin began when she started looking. Some of us run mighty close to that every week. We pay our tithes last—if there's enough money left. That's the same as "looking." It is so easy to think, "If I spend the tithe this week, I can always pay it back next week." The temptation is always there for us to abuse the tithe and remove ourselves from the blessing of God. The moment Adam and Eve ate of that tree, God cast them out. Everything in the Garden became cursed. The moment we begin to partake of the tithe, the moment we touch the thing that God has told us not to touch, the garden of our lives become chaotic. Our finances become cursed. We wonder why Brother So and So's heater lasts ten years while ours only lasts two, or why we only got 20,000 miles out of tires that were supposed to go for 50,000.

The reason is we have touched what God has said "Don't touch." If we don't do things God's way, we have no right to expect Him to bless us. When we do not abide by God's prelude, we are pushed out of His promise. You may be sitting there asking yourself, "I'm a Christian. How come I don't have what I need? How come my kids are always sick? How come we can never get ahead? Why is my marriage in trouble?" It may be that you have touched the forbidden fruit. You may have a management problem in your garden.

God Invests in Good Stock

Before we can hope or expect our overall financial picture to improve, we have to get our priorities straight. Many of us Christians rob ourselves of financial and other kinds of blessings because we have messed up in our management. Some of us tithe faithfully but mismanage the other ninety percent, while others of us can't even bring ourselves to tithe in the first place. It is a sure bet that if we are wrong about the tithe, then we are wrong about the rest of our money. Either way, we lose out on the fullness of the blessings God wants to give us.

As the owner of all things, God has graciously allowed us to manage some of His resources. How much He entrusts to each of us depends on several things: His sovereign will, our willingness to be obedient to Him, and our demonstrated ability as faithful managers of what He has already given. When it comes to investing His wealth and resources, God "plays the stock market."

Some of you undoubtedly have investments of one kind or another. Maybe you invest in the stock market or own real estate. If your investment is not bringing you a good return, what do you do? The answer should be obvious: pull your money out of the unprofitable investment and put it into something that will turn a profit. To do otherwise would be foolish and risky. God is the same way. He invests heavily in those He knows will bring a good return. The amount is not nearly as important as wise and faithful management of that amount.

In Matthew chapter 25, Jesus tells of three servants who were each given different amounts by their master: One received five talents, one received two talents, and one received one talent. The first two servants went out and *immediately* doubled their money through wise investing. Doubling your investment is a good return at any level. The third servant did nothing with his money except hide it. Upon his return from a journey, the master praised the first two servants for their skillful management, but rebuked the third servant for his failure to bring a return. The one talent he had was taken away and given to the first servant, who already had ten. God invests where He knows He will receive a return.

Of course, God's greatest investment in us was sending His Son to die on the cross for our sins and purchase our salvation. He has already invested heavily in us. The question is, what kind of return will we give? God has given each of us something, and we must make the most of any opportunity to do something good with what we have. We need to invest, because we will never have a harvest until we have had seedtime. It is impossible to invest or to make the most of our opportunities if we have touched the Lord's tithe or mismanaged the rest of our resources, because God's curse is already on our endeavors.

Like the three investors of Matthew 25, we are managers—and managers *only*—of what God has entrusted to us, and He holds us responsible for our management. This is true in every area of life, even parenting. Once during a Sunday morning worship service, I (Ken) watched one of the young fathers in our church as he took care of his little boy. He was rocking the child on his lap and praising God with him. As I observed this scene, the thought came to me: "There's the picture. We are managers. Even as parents, we are only managers." God blesses us with children, but they belong to Him. He entrusts them into our care as parents. He has placed these precious young lives in our homes so that we can raise them in the fear and admonition of the Lord. We are responsible for them and God holds us accountable. When we look around and wonder what has gone wrong in our world— teen suicides, school shootings, moral confusion—we need to look no further than ourselves. By and large we have been poor managers of the things that God has given us, whether children or money or anything else.

All through Scripture we find that if we are wise and faithful with what God gives us, He will give us more. God has a wonderful system of doing things. If we are faithful with a little, He will give us a lot. That's not man's philosophy; it's God's Word. To put it in more financial terms, if we invest wisely what we already have, God will give us more to invest. As we said before, God invests in the stock market. Why in the world would He pour talent or wealth into us if He knows that all we will do is bury it in the ground? God is looking for a good investment. He wants a solid return on His resources. Is He looking for more money? No. God does not need more money; He already owns everything. Heaven does not have a cash flow problem. God is simply saying, "I want a return on My investment. I want someone who will finally understand the principle of laying treasures up in Heaven so that when I give them more, they use it to bless and to build My Kingdom. If I can find someone like that, I will have no problem pouring into them."

Here is how it works. The two faithful servants of Matthew 25 made the most of their investment opportunities and doubled their master's money. In return, they received more, a "percentage kickback" so to speak. Now they had their own money to invest and receive a return. In other words, they now had the ability to produce wealth. God will do the same with each of us if we prove faithful with a little. As our investment brings its return, God will return some of that to us as a "kickback" that we can reinvest. We have the ability to produce wealth.

If God wants to bless us so much, why don't we see more of it on a day-to-day basis? Because of our poor management. Imagine a fire hose hooked up to the fire hydrant of Heaven. The water flowing through that hose is all the blessings and resources that God wants to invest in us. He wants to fill us up, but we have put a kink in the hose by failing to understand that we are merely managers and not owners. Through our poor management, and through our touching the forbidden fruit, we have stopped the flow of what God wants to do. God is saying, "I'd love to give you more, but you don't understand why I want to give it. I want you to have it so you can invest in my Kingdom. Instead, you want it for your own selfish pleasure and to gratify your own selfish desires. I can't invest in you unless you are willing to return the kind of increase I am looking for."

Financial Lessons From a Pigsty

Poor management in financial affairs is often the result of selfishness or ignorance. Good financial management is a subject that the Church today sorely needs to address. Too many churches and individual Christians have to make do with a hand-to-mouth existence every day because they have shut off the flow of God's blessings due to poor management. We need to learn how to get the kinks out of the hose. What's more, we need an attitude adjustment in our relationship with material things. There is nothing wrong with having things as long as things do not have us.

Jesus' parable about the prodigal son is one of my favorite stories in the Bible. It comes as the third of three parables dealing with lost things: a lost coin, a lost sheep, and a lost son. Although the primary message of the parable is spiritual in nature, relating to God's willingness to receive and restore those who turn to Him in repentance and faith, the story also contains principles that I believe we can apply to the financial realm.

Like so many of Jesus' parables, the story of the prodigal son involves money:

> *"There was a man who had two sons. The younger one said to his father, 'Father, give me my share of the estate.' So he divided his property between them. Not long after that, the younger son got together all he had, set off for a distant country and there squandered his wealth in wild living. After he had spent everything, there was a severe famine in that whole country, and he began to be in need. So he went and hired himself out to a citizen of that country, who sent him to his fields to feed pigs. He longed to fill his stomach with the pods that the pigs were eating, but no one gave him anything. When he came to his senses, he said, 'How many of my father's hired men have food to spare, and here I am starving to death! I will set out and go back to my father and say to him: Father, I have sinned against heaven and against you. I am no longer worthy to be called your son; make me like one of your hired men.' So he got up and went to his father. But while he was still a long way off, his father saw him and was filled with compassion for him; he ran to his son, threw his arms around him and kissed him.*
>
> *"The son said to him, 'Father, I have sinned against heaven and against you. I am no longer worthy to be called your son.' But the father said to his servants, 'Quick! Bring the best robe and put it on him. Put a ring on his finger and sandals on his feet. Bring the fattened calf and kill it. Let's have a feast and celebrate.*

> *For this son of mine was dead and is alive again; he was lost and is found.' So they began to celebrate."*   Luke 15:11-24

This is a beautiful story and simple, like all of Jesus' parables. A father had two sons. One day the younger son, impatient to be a man, as so many young sons are, came to his father and asked for his inheritance. Traditionally, we have criticized and condemned this young man for making such a request, citing his selfishness and unwillingness to wait until the natural time of inheritance—after his father's death. In reality, however, there was nothing wrong with the son's request; he was simply asking for what was rightfully his. "Father, could you give me the money you've been saving for me?"

If this young man had proven wise in managing his inheritance, we would find no fault in his actions. Would we think of him as a terrible son if he had used his inheritance to feed the hungry or heal the sick or take care of widows and orphans? I don't think so. Because the end result was bad, we tend to think of the whole venture as wrong from the beginning. The son had a legitimate right to request his inheritance. His problems came not because he had money but because he made poor use of it. He had no understanding of the financial principles of investment and multiplication. Young and immature as he was, he probably assumed his wealth would last forever. It didn't. Because of poor management and an undisciplined lifestyle, he quickly squandered his wealth.

It is important that we understand that there is nothing wrong with having an inheritance. There is nothing wrong with a son receiving good things from his father. One of the lessons we need to take from this parable is that *God wants to bless us*. The father in this story was very willing to "divide his property" between his two sons. He wanted them to be prosperous and to do well. Our heavenly Father is the same way. He loves us and wants to shower us with blessings. He wants to flood our lives with good things. Some of us have been beaten down so much by life or have listened to too much wrong preaching and teaching on prosperity that we can't bring ourselves to really believe that God wants to bless us, that He wants to see us prosper.

The parable of the prodigal son pictures God as a loving Father who desires the best for His children. Not only does He bless them abundantly, but He welcomes them back warmly after they have strayed and return in a repentant spirit. He has graciously given us everything we need to succeed. Romans 8:37 says that we are more than conquerors through Christ who loves us. "More than a conqueror" means being *more* than just successful; it means being an overcomer in life. God created us to be the top and not the bottom, the head and not the tail. He created us to prosper at whatever we put our hand to. He planted inside each of us the seed of the ability to produce wealth.

When the younger son left home, he had everything going for him: youth, energy, high hopes and plans, and money. He was full of potential. Sadly, he squandered it all through bad choices and selfish living. Here was a man who not only mismanaged his "ninety percent," but thought nothing of touching God's ten percent and consuming it on his own selfish pleasures and desires. In doing so he brought a curse upon himself and his resources. With no thought for the future and no consideration of his responsibility to God, is it any surprise that he fell on hard times? His state became so low that he was reduced to a job feeding pigs in a sty and so hungry that he was willing to eat what the pigs ate.

There is a lesson here for us. If every day is a financial struggle and you can't seem to make any progress no matter what you do, perhaps you need to examine your attitude and behavior. Like the prodigal son, are you mismanaging your "ninety percent" or, even worse, touching the Lord's tithe—His ten percent? You can't prosper financially if your finances are under a curse because of poor management and bad choices. You won't have any resources to invest in good opportunities that come your way as long as all your money is tied up in debt. It takes money to make money. Money invested is money that multiplies; money that does not multiply does not stay around long.

The prodigal son had everything he needed, but he threw it away and was left destitute. In this we see a second lesson in the story, a principle we have already talked about: *God will never invest more in us than we prove that we are able to handle.* He will never give us ten dollars until we show Him we can handle one dollar. He will never give us a hundred dollars until we show Him we can handle ten dollars. If your finances are not working out right, you need to change something. One definition of insanity is doing the same thing and expecting different results. Take a hard, honest look at your life, your attitude, and your financial habits. Ask the Lord to show you what you need to change and humbly rely on Him for help.

This is what the prodigal son did. His situation became so desperate that he finally came to his senses. Looking around at the muddy sty that was his only shelter and at the dry, empty husks that were his only food, he suddenly realized, "Even my father's servants have it better than this!" Getting up, he headed for home, rehearsing all the way what he would say to his father. He no longer even would claim his rights as a son, which he had done so boldly before. All he would ask would be that he could work as a servant in his father's house. His failure had taught him humility.

His father, however, had other plans. Seeing his son from afar (which indicates that he had been watching for him), the father ran joyfully to welcome his son home and, ignoring the young man's rehearsed speech, reinstated him as a son with full status and privileges as before. This brings us to a third lesson from the pigsty: *even when we have messed up, God can restore us if we come to Him with a repentant heart.*

It is never too late to turn around, never too late to change our behavior. If your finances are in complete disarray, if you are in debt up to your eyeballs, if your wallet or pocketbook is like a sieve in which money pours out faster than it comes in, the Lord can turn your situation around. Don't continue in the same way you have been going and expect anything to change. You have to decide to change. Turn to God in confession and repentance and release control of your financial affairs to Him. Acknowledge to Him your mismanagement of your ninety percent. If necessary, confess to Him your sin of touching the forbidden fruit—of stealing or abusing the Lord's tithe. He will gladly welcome you home and restore you. Your circumstances may not improve drastically overnight; in fact, they probably won't. The road to restoration may be long and will require lots of discipline. Attitudes, habits, and thought patterns usually do not change quickly. The end result, however, will be worth the effort. If you are committed to positive change and to a financial lifestyle that pleases God, He will help you bring it about.

When we talk about Christian financial management, we are talking about *stewardship*. The word *steward* is derived from medieval words: *ste*, which means, "sty" as in a pigsty, and *ward*, which refers to someone who takes care of pigs. In the truest sense of the word, the prodigal son was a steward—a caretaker of pigs. Until he came to his senses and got his attitude straight, pigs were all he could be trusted with. Once he got his life straightened out, things changed. Even though he initially squandered his inheritance, he went from being the steward of a pigsty to being a steward of his father's wealth once again.

It can be the same with us. No matter where you are financially, you don't have to stay there. The Lord can lift you up. He longs to bless you; He just wants to know that He can trust you with His blessings. As long as you are intent on using His blessings for your own selfish desires, you will kink up the hose and shut yourself off from them. If you desire to use your blessings from God to bless others, then He will be glad to channel His blessings through you in increasing measure as you prove faithful. It is all a matter of management.

CHAPTER FIVE

IT'S AUDIT TIME!

Have you ever had your tax returns audited by the IRS? If you have, you already know what a nightmare that can be. We have all heard horror stories about tax audits gone bad. (Is there any other kind?) The auditor examines every exemption, every deduction, every number, every decimal point, every jot and every tittle, of every tax return you filed for the last three years or five years or however many years he is looking at. He expects to see every receipt or documentation for every claimed deduction or exemption. This can be extremely painful and embarrassing, particularly if you are lazy about recordkeeping.

Fear of a tax audit ranks very high on the list of the most common phobias experienced by Americans. Yet, in reality, the chances of any one of us individually being audited is very small. It has been said that we stand a greater chance of getting struck by lightning than we do of having our tax returns audited. Nevertheless, the fear remains very real and very present for many people.

Perhaps this is due at least in part to our general aversion to being held accountable—for anything. We live in a society that loves to pass the buck. No one is responsible for anything; everybody is a victim. If a young man from the inner city commits a crime, the fault lies not with him or with a choice he made, but with his environment. Sexual behaviors and orientations that one generation ago were commonly regarded as immoral or perverse are now seen as merely "alternative lifestyles" that are just as legitimate as any other.

Whether at work or at home or anywhere else, we do not want to be held accountable for our actions. We want to be free to do whatever we wish whenever we wish and not have to worry about any consequences. No matter what happens, someone else is to blame. If our life is messed up, it's someone else's fault. If we barely have enough money to get by every month, it's someone else's fault—the insensitive boss who won't give a raise, the utility company that keeps raising rates, or the credit card companies who charge such high interest.

Buck-passing is nothing new. It has been going on ever since Adam and Eve traded blame in the Garden of Eden. However, if we think we can avoid accountability for our actions and decisions, we are living in a dreamworld. Sometimes accountability is built-in, as in the principles of cause and effect and of action and reaction. If you jump off a bridge, you *will* hit the ground or the water, and it probably won't be pleasant. If you use the money set aside to pay your light bill to buy a television, the day will come when you cannot watch your television because the electric company has turned off your power. Another word for this kind of accountability is *consequences*.

We Will Give an Accounting

One reckoning that we certainly cannot escape is our accountability before God. By creation and design we are managers, and God will hold each of us accountable for our management in every area of life, including financial. It is to our benefit, then, to learn everything we can about good management principles so that we can be faithful stewards of the resources God has given. Fortunately, we have help. The Scriptures speak much about management. Many of Jesus' parables deal with the subject in one way or another. One of these, from the sixteenth chapter of Luke, is one of the most interesting stories in the Bible, at least partly because it contains a couple of unusual twists. Concerning a dishonest steward who is called to task for his stewardship, the parable relates to both management and accountability.

> *Jesus told his disciples: "There was a rich man whose manager was accused of wasting his possessions. So he called him in and asked him, 'What is this I hear about you? Give an account of your management, because you cannot be manager any longer.'*

The manager said to himself, 'What shall I do now? My master is taking away my job. I'm not strong enough to dig, and I'm ashamed to beg—I know what I'll do so that, when I lose my job here, people will welcome me into their houses.' So he called in each one of his master's debtors. He asked the first, 'How much do you owe my master?' 'Eight hundred gallons of olive oil,' he replied. The manager told him, 'Take your bill, sit down quickly, and make it four hundred.' Then he asked the second, 'And how much do you owe?' 'A thousand bushels of wheat,' he replied. He told him, 'Take your bill and make it eight hundred.' The master commended the dishonest manager because he had acted shrewdly. For the people of this world are more shrewd in dealing with their own kind than are the people of the light. I tell you, use worldly wealth to gain friends for yourselves, so that when it is gone, you will be welcomed into eternal dwellings. Whoever can be trusted with very little can also be trusted with much, and whoever is dishonest with very little will also be dishonest with much. So if you have not been trustworthy in handling worldly wealth, who will trust you with true riches? And if you have not been trustworthy with someone else's property, who will give you property of your own? No servant can serve two masters. Either he will hate the one and love the other, or he will be devoted to the one and despise the other. You cannot serve both God and Money."   Luke 16:1-13

First of all, a rich man called his manager to account after hearing a disturbing report: Someone had accused the manager of wasting his master's possessions. The accusation must have had merit, because the rich man decided to fire the manager: "Give an account of your management, because you cannot be manager any longer." Audit time came and the manager was caught short. If God audited your bank account today, would He accuse you of wasting His possessions? Would He tell you to give Him an account of your management?

God will call all of us one day. The time will come when each of us must give an account to God of our management—our stewardship of what He entrusted to us. Parents, we will have to give God an account of how we raised our children. Did we raise them to know and fear and love God? Did we teach them how to live righteous and holy lives in the power of the Holy Spirit? Did we prepare them to live God-honoring lives of service?

Another important balance sheet on that day will be how we used our time. Did we use our time for the Lord? That is why we need to learn now how to be good stewards of our time. If we are faithful in our stewardship of time, God will help us produce more in one day than most people do in a week.

Don't forget talents. God will hold us accountable for *everything* He gave us. Maybe you can sing like an angel but won't use your talent in the church because you don't want to submit to the leadership. Perhaps you feel that your talents are not important enough or developed enough to use for God. You may be saying, "I need to wait until I have some training." Don't wait; begin now. Of course, if you can get training, certainly take advantage of it. In the meantime, though, start right away being faithful with the little God has given you, and He will give you more. When you prove faithful with the little He gives you to start with, He will then begin to give you a little bit more and a little bit more and a little bit more until He brings you into a fullness of wisdom and experience. Even then, you will not have "arrived." You will need to continue to reinvest what God has given you so that you can give Him a good return on His investment.

God will also call us to give an account of our financial stewardship. What did we do with the resources He gave us? How did we spend our money? What did we invest in? What was our attitude and practice with regard to giving? Were we faithful with the tithe? Were we faithful in seeking His will for the other ninety percent? Did we give priority to His Kingdom work or to our own pursuits? If life is a daily struggle for you because you cannot make ends meet, you need to ask yourself why. Remember, God invests great wealth only in those who prove faithful with little wealth. Take a close look at your own situation. If God called on you today, what kind of accounting would you be able to give?

Be Careful Who You Give Money To

Giving is an important part of stewardship, but good stewardship calls for responsible giving. This means that although we should never ignore the indigent, the homeless, the hungry, or others in need, we should not necessarily give to every person who walks through the door. If good stewardship involves responsible giving, responsible giving requires discernment. Unfortunately, some people who have genuine needs will bleed our resources dry if we let them. Giving to people who make no effort to change their circumstances but who live constantly off the goodwill of others is like throwing our corn on the gravel. It consumes resources that could be put to better and wider use elsewhere.

Discernment is important also because it is physically impossible for us to give to each and every legitimate need that comes to our attention. That is when we must ask the Lord to reveal the specific needs that we should invest in.

There is another side to the coin. Don't support every preacher or evangelist who comes on television, because many of them are not worthy of support. Some folks think they have an anointing just because they have a television ministry. Many Christians give more money to televangelists than they do to their own local churches. Before you contribute a dime to a television ministry or a parachurch organization or any other such entity, consider this: You are accountable to God for what you do with your money, but who are these folks accountable to? How will they use your money if they get it? How will you know if your money has been used the way you intended? Short of receiving a financial statement from them, there is no real way to know.

Please understand. There is nothing at all wrong with giving gifts; just be sure you know who you are giving to, what they stand for, and how your gift will be used. Whatever you do, don't give a gift because someone has manipulated you. Some slick preacher in a thousand-dollar suit begs for money saying, "Give generously, and God will supply all your needs." If it is true that God will supply all our needs (and it is—see Philippians 4:19) why doesn't that fancy preacher take his own advice and trust God to supply all of *his* needs instead of begging us for our money?

A good attitude to adopt is to realize that whenever you give, you are giving not to a preacher or a ministry or an organization, but to God. If you have prayed and exercised discernment and given great care to your decision, once you have given your gift, let it go. After your gift leaves your hand, don't worry about it. You gave it to the Lord. If the person or ministry to which you gave misuses your money, that is between them and God. After all, it's not your money anyway, or theirs; it's God's money. If they have offended God by misusing your gift, He can deal with the problem much better than you can. The fleas of a thousand camels will find their armpits. You can't direct fleas, but God can. It's God's problem and He will take care of it. Your responsibility is to be careful, discerning, and faithful. So, give your gift and let go of it.

Any responsible ministry or Christian organization should be up front and open with its finances. It should be easy to obtain a copy of the financial records of receipts and expenditures so that those who contribute can see how responsibly their contributions have been used. If the organization is secretive about these things, steer clear of it. If it has nothing to hide, then why hide anything?

At the end of every year, our church has its annual business meeting. At that time, members can see how every penny that came into the church during the previous year was used. All the financial matters of the church are up front and out in the open. There is no way that anyone could misappropriate any funds, because a board oversees every dollar that is spent.

Wouldn't you rather invest in someone or something that you can get your hands on and who will make themselves accountable to those who give them support? You are accountable to God for your financial stewardship. Be careful who you give money to.

Find Creative Solutions

Returning to Jesus' parable of the dishonest steward, we find in Luke 16:3 that the steward faced a dilemma: "What shall I do now? My master is taking away my job. I'm not strong enough to dig, and I'm ashamed to beg." It didn't take long for his quick, shrewd mind to come up with a solution. He decided on a scheme that would make people feel indebted to him so that when he needed their help, they would take him in. Basically, he went down the list of people who owed his master money, called them in, and gave them each a generous price break. One man who owed for eight hundred gallons of olive oil was only charged for four hundred gallons; another who was in debt for one thousand bushels of wheat only had to pay for eight hundred bushels.

The next scripture, verse eight, has to be one of the oddest verses of the whole Bible: "The master commended the dishonest manager because he had acted shrewdly. For the people of this world are more shrewd in dealing with their own kind than are the people of the light." Remember, this is Jesus speaking. His disciples are gathered around Him listening intently like kindergartners sitting on their mats during story time. Jesus says that the master *commended* the dishonest steward for his shrewdness. Why? It would be one thing if the verse said that the master commended his manager; there's nothing wrong with that. Why, however, did the master commend his *dishonest* steward, and what is Jesus' point for including this detail in the story? It sounds almost as though the steward is being commended and praised for his dishonest behavior.

One key to understanding this is found in the last part of the verse: "For the people of this world are more shrewd in dealing with their own kind than are the people of the light." We could discuss and debate all day the nature of the dishonest steward's actions. Perhaps he originally overbilled his master's clients, or maybe he was guilty of embezzling his master's money. We will never know, because the text does not tell us. Besides, the exact nature of his dishonesty is not important. The point that Jesus is making is that just as the people in the world are usually creative enough to find solutions to their problems, so the people of God ought to learn to deal shrewdly also. In other words, Jesus is saying that when worldly people have a problem, they figure out a solution. Granted, their solution may involve cheating, lying, or stealing, but they *do* find a solution, and it is often a very creative solution.

The master commended the dishonest steward not so much for his dishonesty but for his creativity in solving the problem of his imminent unemployment. His solution was to do a favor for his master's clients so that they would do him a favor after he was out of a job by taking him into their home, perhaps even hiring him as *their* manager. At any rate, he would be off the street and not destitute. This is the old "you scratch my back and I'll scratch yours" arrangement.

With shrewdness and creativity the dishonest steward solved a potentially serious personal dilemma. The same should be true of us. Of all people, we who are the people of God should be able to find creative solutions to our problems. After all, God the Creator made us in His own image, which means that we are creative by nature.

Deuteronomy 8:18 says that God has given us the creative ability to produce wealth. Jesus' point is that if the world can be creative and shrewd in problem solving, we Christians should be even better at coming up with creative (but legal and honest) ways to get ourselves out of debt. If the world can figure out a way, how much more should we as children of light who carry the anointing of God be able to find ways to break free from financial bondage?

Misappropriation

Jesus' parable of the dishonest steward never states specifically what he did to "waste" his master's possessions, but we can safely assume that his actions involved misappropriation of funds in one form or another. The word *misappropriation* means, "to wrongly apply or to use without authority." That is exactly where so many of us get into trouble, particularly where the tithe is concerned. It is also one of the main reasons why so many Christians, whether tithers or not, still live a hand-to-mouth existence. Whenever we steal or withhold the tithe, we misappropriate. Whenever we use any of our financial resources in ways that displease God or grieve His Spirit, we misappropriate. Whenever we "lay claim" to money as our own and use it with no thought for God's desires, we misappropriate. We cannot misuse God's money one day and then expect Him to bless us the next.

Every penny, every dime, every dollar that we have belongs to God. We need to acknowledge God's authority concerning how we spend our money. God might say, "I want you to do thus and so," but we cannot because we have already used the money for something else. We want God to bless us over here, but He cannot because we have not done what He asked us to do over there. Blessing requires obedience—with one hundred percent, not just ten percent.

Tithing is a biblical act of worship, obedience, and honor that acknowledges God as the owner of all things. Ten percent given directly to the Lord and His work does not mean the other ninety percent is "free" money for us to use any way we please. The tithe reminds us that *all* of our money and other financial resources are under God's ownership and subject to His will and desire. It is easy to develop a legalistic attitude about the tithe, feeling that once we have tithed we have done our financial duty to God. In reality, we should think of our tithe as the bottom line, the minimum that we ought to give.

An even higher principle is to give as we have been blessed. In other words, let the degree of our blessing determine the degree of our giving. After all, the New Testament tells us to give *everything*. Throughout the centuries, some Christians have interpreted this literally and taken a vow of poverty. More likely, this means to hold everything we possess with a light grip. Give the tithe faithfully and cheerfully, and place everything else at God's disposal.

Jesus concludes the parable of the dishonest steward with some instructions regarding our use of money. He says in Luke 16:9: "I tell you, use worldly wealth to gain friends for yourselves, so that when it is gone, you will be welcomed into eternal dwellings." What on earth does He mean here? This verse is almost as surprising as verse 8 in that on the surface it seems to suggest that we should use our money to buy friends. Surely that cannot be what Jesus means! We studied commentary after commentary and read this verse in every translation we could get our hands on in an effort to understand what Jesus is saying. In essence, Jesus is saying that we should seek to use our money in such a way that others will be brought into the Kingdom of God. We need to understand that we are blessed in order to be a blessing. Otherwise, our blessing will turn into a curse. Misappropriation of God's money not only shuts us off from His blessing, but also everyone else He wanted to bless through us. Let's take seriously the money we have from God. How we use it is a great privilege, but it also carries a great responsibility.

Monopoly

So far we have dealt with the management of money and the misappropriation of money. Now we need to look at another common problem: the *monopoly* of money. The remainder of Luke chapter 16 is devoted to another parable of Jesus, the story of a selfish rich man and a poor beggar named Lazarus. In this story the rich man monopolizes his wealth, using it for his own pleasure and comfort, either unaware or unconcerned that he could have used his wealth to be a blessing to others. One day God turned the tables.

"There was a rich man who was dressed in purple and fine linen and lived in luxury every day. At his gate was laid a beggar named Lazarus, covered with sores and longing to eat what fell

from the rich man's table. Even the dogs came and licked his sores. The time came when the beggar died and the angels carried him to Abraham's side. The rich man also died and was buried. In hell, where he was in torment, he looked up and saw Abraham far away, with Lazarus by his side. So he called to him, 'Father Abraham, have pity on me and send Lazarus to dip the tip of his finger in water and cool my tongue, because I am in agony in this fire.' But Abraham replied, 'Son, remember that in your lifetime you received your good things, while Lazarus received bad things, but now he is comforted here and you are in agony. And besides all this, between us and you a great chasm has been fixed, so that those who want to go from here to you cannot, nor can anyone cross over from there to us.' He answered, 'Then I beg you, father, send Lazarus to my father's house, for I have five brothers. Let him warn them, so that they will not also come to this place of torment.' Abraham replied, 'They have Moses and the Prophets; let them listen to them.' 'No, father Abraham,' he said, 'but if someone from the dead goes to them, they will repent.' He said to him, 'If they do not listen to Moses and the Prophets, they will not be convinced even if someone rises from the dead.'" Luke 16:19-31

Have you ever played the game of Monopoly? Don't you just hate that game? Everybody else buys all the properties before you can get to them! By the time you get around the board, the other players are charging you. Monopoly is one of the meanest games you can learn as a kid. It's dog-eat-dog from the word go. There is nothing spiritual about it at all. He who has the most money wins.

Unlike the board game, we need to be careful that we don't begin to monopolize our money in real life. This is true with our personal finances as well as our corporate finances in the church. In our church, there is always something to build, somebody to reach, something else to do. Even in the midst of great building programs, however, we do not use one hundred percent of our money on ourselves. We continue to advance in giving to missions. We will never put missionary support on hold. We will never put outreaches on hold. We will never slow down in the area of evangelism.

Sometimes we can come dangerously close to monopolizing our

finances by getting so caught up in them that we fail to see or ignore the needs around us. That's what happened with the rich man in Jesus' parable. Day after day he passed right by poor Lazarus begging right outside his gate and never gave him a second thought. This story describes the peril of being rich in the things of the world but poor in the things of God. When the rich man died, he had nothing laid up in Heaven because he had ignored his seed on earth. He never planted for the future; he never invested for the good of others. Rather than being a godly manager, he misappropriated his wealth, considering it all as belonging to him rather than to God, and monopolized it all for himself. In the end, he found himself tormented in hell, while Lazarus received his rest and reward "at Abraham's side" (a metaphor for Heaven or Paradise).

Like the rich man, we sometimes fall into the trap of wanting to hoard our money. Material wealth can be addictive. Only by keeping our priorities straight and understanding our identity as stewards, not owners, can we avoid being sucked in by the allure of worldly wealth. Once we understand that the purpose of God's blessings is not for our own selfish consumption but to in turn bless others, we will take a different view toward money. We will see money not as an end in itself but as a tool to help the needy and enrich the lives of other people, leaving a legacy that will bless future generations.

Let's look at two modern examples as a lesson in contrasts: the lives and legacies of F. W. Woolworth and Milton S. Hershey. These two American businessmen were among the wealthiest men of their day, but they were poles apart in their attitude toward their wealth and what they did with it. Many of us remember the chain of Woolworth stores that stretched across the country; the original "five and dime" stores. Throughout his career, F. W. Woolworth devoted himself to building more stores and turning a profit no matter what the cost, and the cost was high. He virtually neglected his family. His family life was atrocious. His primary interest was making a name for himself in the business world, and he did. His biggest problem was that he confused his net worth with his self-worth. That is a trap all of us need to be very careful about, thinking we are *somebody* just because we have a business card and a big bank account.

F. W. Woolworth's last goal was achieved in 1913 when he erected a skyscraper that was to be the monument to his success. At his death,

Woolworth was worth millions and millions of dollars, yet he left no money to charity or to anyone else outside his family. He left no lasting legacy of his time on earth. His fortune went to the members of his immediate family who, in turn, got into all kinds of trouble and destroyed the family's financial empire. In 1997, Woolworth stores across America went out of business. The following year the Woolworth Building in New York City, at the time of its construction the tallest skyscraper in the world, was sold. The business that F. W. Woolworth had devoted his life to disappeared, and the name Woolworth essentially vanished from history.

Woolworth's story reminds us of the words of Solomon in Ecclesiastes 5:15-16: "Naked a man comes from his mother's womb, and as he comes, so he departs. He takes nothing from his labor that he can carry in his hand. This too is a grievous evil: As a man comes, so he departs, and what does he gain, since he toils for the wind?" All of us come into this world with nothing and we leave with nothing. It is what we do in between that makes the difference. By wise investing, by generous giving, by responsible management, and by refusing to monopolize our resources we can lay up for ourselves treasures in Heaven. We can leave a legacy that will bless millions long after we are gone. This is a truth that Milton S. Hershey understood.

Milton S. Hershey—that's right, the maker of the Hershey candy bar—measured his success in how his wealth could help others. He had no children of his own, yet left his entire fortune to a foundation that created a school for underprivileged children. Part of his financial legacy included a world-class medical center that specializes in many kinds of cutting-edge medical treatment and research and has brought the blessing of physical healing to countless people from around the world. The Hershey company, founded over a century ago, is still a growing and thriving business today, not just in candy, but in the larger food industry. Hershey Foods is consistently one of the top five hundred stocks in America. All of this from a man who had a dream of making a better chocolate bar, as well as a spirit of generosity that expanded far beyond the dimensions of his own life.

How winners and losers are determined is different in God's economics than it is in ours. It is *quality* of financial management that matters, not *quantity*. God is more interested in *how* than in *how much*. As we have already said many times, the issue is attitude, not *amount*.

What are we doing with our finances? Why are so many Christians so far in debt that they couldn't help somebody if their life depended on it?

If you are in debt, we're not trying to make you feel bad, but we hope you get angry enough to do something about it. God has called us to be good stewards, and that means we should produce. Our investments ought to bring good returns. God has given us the ability to do it. Here is what it amounts to: *If you and I don't finance the end-time revival, who will?*

Financial freedom rarely comes overnight. It is just like life: no thunderbolts, just line upon line and precept upon precept, a little here and a little there. In the end it will be faithfulness and obedience that win the day. Part of the process of freedom is getting rid of false teachings and ideas about finances. It is time to take a look at some honest facts about money as well as some common myths about money that often trip us up.

Chapter Six

Honest Facts About Christians and Money

The Church ought to be in charge. We ought to control our own destiny. We shouldn't have to go groveling and begging to somebody else. There is no reason why the Church—not to mention individual Christians—should be subservient to banks, loan institutions, or other secular financial bodies. As children of the King of kings, we ought to be the lenders rather than the borrowers and the leaders rather than the followers. Something is terribly wrong when the Church is constantly playing catch-up with the world. We should be at the forefront of creative service, innovative strategies, and humble ministry. When was the last time society or the government looked to the Church for the cue of where to go and what to do? In the minds of many in our culture, the Church—and its message—has become irrelevant.

It's amazing. We have Christians who can't even take a day off of work to go to a conference or a workshop or a training event somewhere because they are so bound by debt that they have to put in every extra hour they can just to pay the installments. Some feel they can't even take time off to spend with their families. We are working more hours, spending more money, and for what? Financially, America is better off today than at almost any time in our history. There is more money on these shores than ever before, yet individual Americans have less money in personal savings accounts than ever before. It would seem most Americans, if struck with a tragedy or disaster, could live no more than a month on their savings. Christians are in the same boat as everybody else.

God did not plan for or ordain things to be this way. His plan has always been for His people to prosper as an example for the rest of the world. The reason so many of us do not is due to many factors: ignorance, false assumptions about money and finances, bad choices, disobedience, sin in our lives, and unholy lifestyles. We flirt with the world and shut ourselves off from God's abundant provision and blessing. In spite of Jesus' admonitions to the contrary, we seek to serve both God and money.

Does any of this stir your spirit? Good! If your financial "boat" is leaking, we want to provoke you into doing something about it! We challenge you to stand up in the presence of God and say, "Lord, with your help, I am going to be a faithful steward, starting right now." If you say that and mean it, God will honor your decision and bless you.

What does it mean to say that the Church should be in charge, that Christians should be leaders rather than followers? We believe Christians could be the CEOs of big multimillion-dollar corporations. By applying God's financial principles to our businesses as well as our homes, we ought to be able to prove ourselves so wise and prudent and such good stewards that when the time comes to name a new CEO or a new president or a new manager, those charged with the selection will pick us over everybody else. There should be such an anointing, such a presence of God, in our lives that we rise to the top of the list of most-qualified candidates. Is that too far beyond our imagination? Anything is possible with God.

Christians ought to get promoted. If we are to be promoted, however, we must learn to work as unto God. That means working hard even when the boss isn't around. It means being a self-starter, a self-motivator, an innovator. It means being as good a steward with somebody else's time and money as we are with our own, if not better. As Christians, we should have a different motivation and a different work ethic than unbelievers. We should work not because the boss is nearby but because we want to honor the Lord with our labor and our faithfulness.

If you are hired to paint a building, aim for more than just doing a job to get a paycheck. Paint that building as though you were painting God's house. In our daily lives, in our work ethic, and in every aspect of our behavior, people should see the presence of God. The witness of our life and attitude helps them see a way that works better than their way, a life more satisfying than theirs. They may never openly acknowledge the difference as due to the presence of God, but they may say, "You know, there is something different about you. There seems to be some kind of favor on your life. What's up?" Many times, the way we live our lives will open more doors to talk about Jesus than any amount of words we could say.

Don't Be a Phony

That is why it is critically important that we be up-front, honest, and absolutely genuine all the time. There should be no hint, no trace of phoniness in our speech, attitude, or behavior. One way we can grow in this area is to practice discernment.

Be genuine on your job. Pray about your attitude and behavior in the workplace. Ask God to give you discernment. Develop boldness. Put ideas in the suggestion box and sign your name in large letters. After all, nothing ventured, nothing gained. The worst that could happen is having your idea rejected. Who knows? Your suggestion might be just the ticket that management has been looking for to improve productivity or profit margin. That is when they will start to take notice of you.

Be genuine at home. You should be the same at home as you are in public. Your family should never have to cover up for you because your private persona is so different from your public face. This means being a person of integrity. The word *integrity* is related to the word *integrated* in the sense of everything working smoothly together as a unified whole. Being genuine means having no inconsistencies in speech or behavior.

Be genuine at church and in your private walk with God. God already knows everything about you, so why put on a face? The church should be a place where we can feel secure enough to let our guard down and be ourselves. Too often it is the opposite. We put on a façade at church because we are terrified of people finding out who we really are or that we don't really have it all together, and that they will not like us because of it. Don't be afraid to talk about money at church. Money and its management are legitimate spiritual topics, and need to be addressed in a wise and discerning manner. Be faithful with your tithe, not out of duty but as an act of worship and devotion. By tithing ten percent, you are making a public statement to others that God is in charge of all of your money. Everything is just a multiple of ten anyway. When you give ten percent, you symbolize that you are giving *everything* to God. People are watching. Don't give *because* they are watching, but let the knowledge that they are watching humble you into praying that God be honored and glorified by your example.

When we are faithful to God financially, He draws a circle around our house, our cars, and all our other "stuff" and says, "That's Mine, devil; you can't touch it. Devil, leave that furnace alone." Those tires that were only supposed to go 50,000 miles will now go 60,000. If the Israelites could walk around in the desert for forty years in one pair of sandals, God can certainly take care of our assets. Trust Him. Tithing is trust in action.

Be genuine in your relationships with others, and particularly with unbelievers. Most people can spot a phony a mile away. For example, what good does it do to come to church and get all excited in worship and sing and shout and dance to the Lord and praise Him for supplying all your needs when your marriage stinks, your kids are uncontrollable, and you can't balance your checkbook? What message do we send to the world when they look at us and say, "There goes Bob. He's a deacon down at the church. Did you hear he's filing for bankruptcy?" Or, "I just found out that Rev. Darcy had his new car repossessed." We understand that tragedies happen; however, many times they can be avoided with better stewardship.

We invite people to church, but they are offended because we haven't paid our bills. We beg for money to pay bills while at the same time proclaiming that God will supply all our needs. No wonder the lost world looks at us and says, "You're a phony."

God is concerned about *every* area of our lives. He's concerned with more than just getting us filled with the Holy Spirit. I know people who are filled with the Holy Spirit who are absolutely stupid in their finances. There is a difference between ignorance and stupidity. Ignorance means we don't know any better. Stupidity is knowing better but not doing it. It's great to be filled with the Holy Spirit, but we also need to be responsible in every area of life, including finances. Don't be a phony. Don't act like you know something if you don't. Be open and honest. Ask questions. With all the information readily available today on finances or any other conceivable subject, there is no excuse for ignorance.

We Can't Afford Financial Ignorance

When it comes to finances, we can't afford to be ignorant. If you don't know anything about finances, make it a priority to learn. Talk to a professional financial counselor or a trusted friend or family member who has knowledge in these areas. Attend a financial seminar. More and more churches are beginning to offer them as they recognize the importance of their people being financially astute. Quite often they are free and the quality of information excellent. You can learn about investments: good ones, bad ones, and how to tell the difference. You can learn about stocks and bonds. What is a stock? What is a bond? How do they work? How does the stock market operate? You can learn about mutual funds: what they are and how they work. You can learn how to plan for retirement or how to start a savings plan no matter what your income level. You can even learn practical and workable ways to get out of debt.

All the financial information any of us need is readily available through many different sources, a far cry from just a generation ago when these subjects were the domain of bankers and financiers, and when nonprofessionals like most of us had to learn by trial and error. Do whatever it takes to gain financial knowledge. The apostle Paul said that ignorance separates us from the blessings of God. As I said before, ignorance means we don't know any better. At the same time, ignorance will not excuse us from our responsibility as stewards before God. Ignorant or not, we are accountable. Ignorance of the law really is no excuse. That being true, let us avail ourselves of every opportunity to gain knowledge. Ignorance will keep us in financial bondage, while knowledge will set us free. Wouldn't it be tragic to miss out on the blessings of God simply because nobody ever told us?

Let Your Faith Work

Here is a foundational statement for finances or any other area in life: *Faith will work if you work it.* Noah believed God about a great flood coming, but he still had to pick up his hammer and ax and build the ark. Abraham believed God's promise that he would become the father of a mighty nation, but he still had to offer his son Isaac as a sacrifice to the Lord.

Faith will work if you work it. What exactly does that mean? It comes down to this: Belief is one thing, but belief that gets results is another. We have to put our faith into action. Sometimes we Christians develop a "lottery" mindset: "One day my ship will come in. Someday everything will all come together for me." We get the idea that the only way we will ever be financially prosperous is for some unexpected windfall to come our way, such as winning the lottery or a big sweepstakes or receiving an inheritance from a rich relative. One of the popular television shows of recent years was *Who Wants to Be a Millionaire?* where contestants could win a million dollars simply by answering successfully a series of increasingly challenging questions. Millions of people tuned in because becoming a millionaire seems to be everybody's dream.

There is a better, more reliable way to become a millionaire, if that is what you want. Learning and following sound financial principles regarding savings, investments, budgeting, and debt will over time produce wealth. Many of these principles are found in the Word of God. Success involves not only knowing the principles, but being disciplined in following them day after day and week after week until they work, and then to keep on going. People who start following these principles while in their twenties or early thirties can be millionaires by the time they are fifty or sixty years old.

Faith will work if you work it. Just remember that faith is a *walk*, not a sprint, a *journey*, not a destination. Success begins small, like a seed planted, and gradually grows until an abundant harvest comes in. It is highly unlikely that you will ever have a harvest unless you first plant a seed. There really is no such thing as an overnight success. Some successes appear that way because much careful preparation and diligent, disciplined effort was expended for years far away from the limelight. When success finally came, it appeared to be sudden but was actually the fruit of the careful nurturing of a seed planted long before.

Faith will work if you work it. If you want corn, you have to plant a kernel in the ground. That's a start, but alone it is not enough. You have to work it, nurture it, water it, fertilize it, hoe it, get rid of the weeds, and keep the birds away—not just once but every day for months. Eventually, that one kernel will produce a harvest of corn.

Working faith requires patience, a willingness to work hard, and above all, *discipline*. Some Christians walk around saying, "Someday, God is going to help me be a prayer warrior." With that kind of thinking, it will probably never happen. We simply don't do the obvious in order to reach our goals. Imagine if you had a friend who asked you to be his accountability partner by calling him at six o'clock every morning to wake him up to pray. Wouldn't you tell that person, "Absolutely not! That's the dumbest thing I ever heard. First of all, I'm not getting up just for your convenience because I might not be getting up at six o'clock that day." Suppose he then said, "Well then, would you pray that God would wake me up?" "No," you would and should answer, "I'm not going to pray that God would wake you up either. That's what alarm clocks are for. Set the alarm clock. When it goes off, get your lazy self out of bed." The obvious thing for this friend to do would be to simply set his alarm every morning and to keep his commitment to praying at that time.

Sometimes we Christians pray some of the dumbest prayers. "Oh, God, help me to get up." Get your own self up. Faith will work if you work it. You say you want to be a prayer warrior? Then get up and work your faith. You want to have a good marriage? Then work on your marriage. You want to be a good parent? Then work on being a good parent. Search the Scriptures and find the principles that will help you in these things. You want to produce wealth? Then put some money away. Stop spending everything that God invests in you so that it won't simply dwindle away. Otherwise, when windows of opportunity open they won't open for you because, you don't have two dollars to rub together.

Faith will work if you work it. If you remember nothing else from this book, remember that. Faith will work if you work it, and that applies to every category of life. It will work in your marriage, in your parenting, in your career, in your finances, and in your spiritual walk. If you want revival, stop praying for God to show up in a lightning bolt and start a fire on the altar. We hear so much about praying for God to "show up." I've got news for you, friends. God is not going to show up. He's already here. If you want revival, work your faith. Faith will work if you work it.

Faith is not some mystical thing. Faith is evidence. Hebrews 11:1

says, "Now faith is the substance of things hoped for, the evidence of things not seen" (KJV). A court of law relies on evidence, not hearsay. You can't get up in a court of law and say, "Well, I just have this feeling…" or "I was meditating…." No. Solid evidence is the only acceptable testimony.

Faith is evidence. Faith is to the spiritual world what money is to the physical world. In the physical world, money allows us to go and take possession of something we need, whether food or clothing or whatever. Similarly, faith enables us to take possession of whatever we need in the spiritual realm. Faith and finances are closely related. If our finances are going to be blessed, it is going to take faith. That is not just sitting back and saying, "Okay, God, rain on me," and expecting dollar bills to come floating down from Heaven. No. Faith is evidence, which means that there is something tangible in the Word of God that will purchase the thing that we are hoping for. Faith is the substance of things hoped for and the evidence of things not seen.

Reach Over the Wall

When it comes to the Church's relationship with the world, the Church should be leading the way, setting the example. We need to "reach over the wall." Joseph, son of Jacob, rose from being a slave in Egypt, and for a while a prisoner in the dungeon, to being named prime minister of Egypt, second only to Pharaoh. His steadfast faith in God enabled him not only to be a wise and capable administrator, but also to be instrumental in saving the people of Egypt from the effects of a devastating famine. Sometime later, Jacob, his father, speaking prophetic words over each of his twelve sons, said of Joseph, "Joseph is a fruitful vine, a fruitful vine near a spring, whose branches climb over a wall" (Genesis 49:22). That metaphor means that wherever Joseph was planted—in the slave quarters, in the prison, in Pharaoh's court—he was able to affect and influence those on the other side of the wall. In other words, Joseph made a difference wherever he was, and whatever the setting.

Joseph is a picture of what the Church should be. We should make a difference wherever we are, wherever we are planted. The Church should be in the vanguard of compassionate service and ministry in society. Our thoughts and ideas on ethics, morality, and spirituality should set the tone of public discussion. We should always be pressing ahead, staying a few steps in front, being the pacesetter for society rather than the trend-follower. When government leaders are looking for a way to improve social services, they ought to be able to look at the Church and model their programs after our example. If they want a better way to feed the hungry or shelter the homeless, they should be able to draw lessons from the Church because we are already doing it.

If we as the Church are ever going to reach those who are on the other side, we have got to exercise God's principles. How are we going to reach the top CEOs in the country? We have to reach over the wall. If we ever hope to draw in other people besides just a bunch of church folks who come in every Sunday for their weekly spiritual "pep rally," we are going to have to reach over the wall. Joseph reached over the wall and, by exercising God's principles of leadership and stewardship, saved not only his own family but an entire nation as well. At the time that Moses led the Israelites out of Egypt, over 400 years after the days of Joseph, Egypt was a very wealthy nation. Her great affluence was due in no small part to Joseph's leadership and influence. The destinies of nations are directly linked to the godliness (or ungodliness) of their leaders. As prime minister of Egypt, Joseph followed God's plan, and God in turn blessed the nation.

As a couple of guys who were once down and outers, we have a heart to reach the down and outers. We want to feed those who need to be fed and to clothe those who need to be clothed. At the same time, we would love to reach some of those CEOs sitting in their leather and mahogany offices atop corporate skyscrapers and thinking they have need of nothing. It will never happen unless we can learn from Paul to reach over the wall and "become all things to all men so that by all possible means [we] might save some" (1 Corinthians 9:22). Most of them want nothing to do with the Church because, at least in part, we have communicated the message that being spiritual means being poor.

Look at it from their perspective. If they see us serving God faithfully and yet barely getting by financially, why would they want what we have? If you asked them, they might say, "Who wants your God? What kind of a God leaves His people to squeak by, barely surviving from day to day, and having to stand in bread and cheese lines? I want nothing to do with it." I know that doesn't sound very spiritual, but we need to understand that this is the way they think. We shouldn't expect unspiritual people to think in spiritual terms. We must learn to think the way they think if we want to reach who they reach. People with money need Jesus too. One significant reason for getting our financial house in order, both individually and collectively, is so we can reach over the wall.

Six Reasons Why Christians Ought to Have Money

When was the last time you heard anyone say that Christians are *supposed* to have money? We are not supposed to *live* for money, but we do need money to finance the work of God's Kingdom. Money is the mechanism for getting things done in the world. There really is power in money, either godly power or satanic power. The more Christians who have money and are committed to godly stewardship, the more money will be available for the Lord's work and the less for the devil's. After all, the Bible says that the wealth of the wicked has been set aside for the righteous.

We want to share with you six reasons why Christians ought to have money. There are probably many more, but these are pretty basic.

1. To use for God's glory and God's purposes. God will not bless us with wealth to consume on our own arrogance and selfish desires. He does not give us money just so we can satisfy our lusts. God gives us money so we can be partners with Him in turning it to redemptive uses in the world around us. He blesses us so we can bless others.

2. There is nothing wrong with Christians having nice things. Nothing in the Bible ever states or implies that it is wrong for believers to have wealth. As long as you are paying your tithe, honoring God with the other ninety percent, giving to missions, and helping the needy, then we say, "Go for it!" Don't be embarrassed or ashamed. We know a pastor who lives in a million-dollar home, drives a Mercedes, and has a vacation condo. He is really hooked up. It would be very easy to look at him and say, "That's terrible! How can he be a man of God?" First of all, why is it okay for a CEO of an ungodly company to make millions, yet a pastor who oversees people's souls can't have anything? Why can't he take nice vacations or have a swimming pool in his backyard?

Sometimes we are so quick to judge without giving a thought to the facts behind the situation. Many of us have grown up with wrong perceptions of how Christians—and clergy in particular—ought to live. Big, fancy house—no way. Fine luxury car—not a chance. Why not? That's the question nobody really has a good answer for. I (Ken) have always enjoyed cars. When I first got into the ministry, I bought a Cadillac. I thought the folks in my church were going to crucify me! What they didn't know was that I had bought the car at an auction for $2,000. Only four years old, someone had stolen it, taken it for a joyride, and blown the engine. After I bought the car, a buddy of mine put a brand, new engine in it for a little over $1,000. Now I had a four-year-old Cadillac with a new engine that I had invested only $3,500 in, yet a lot of folks in the church had a problem with it. In the end, I sold the Cadillac and bought a more expensive car that was not seen as a status symbol of wealth.

We need to be very careful about our perceptions and our prejudices. Kept in perspective, there is nothing wrong with Christians—including clergy—having wealth or enjoying nice things.

3. So that we can loan and not borrow. We have already talked about this one a little. Remember Proverbs 22:7: "The rich rule over the poor, and the borrower is servant to the lender." Deuteronomy 15:6 says, "For the LORD your God will bless you as he has promised, and you will lend to many nations but will borrow from none. You will rule over many nations but none will rule over you." How can we help others financially if all our money is tied up in paying back those who have loaned to us? This brings us to the next one.

4. So we can be Good Samaritans. We need money so that we can help people in distress and others in need. Could the Good Samaritan have walked down that road, picked up the wounded man, put him on a donkey, taken him to the inn, and paid for his care if he did not have financial resources available for such use? Neither could we.

5. For retirement. In today's changed work world, we can't depend on the expectation of career-long employment with one company. Retirement plans are not the same as they used to be. We need money so we can set up our own retirement.

6. For college. Some of you may not need or want college money for yourself, but what about your children or your grandchildren? Proverbs 13:22 says, "A good man leaves an inheritance for his children's children, but a sinner's wealth is stored up for the righteous." If you have preschoolers or school-age children, now is the time to start some kind of college fund. It doesn't have to be big in the beginning—even ten dollars a week is better than nothing. The important thing is to do something, and to start now.

Ten Money Myths—Plus One

One of the most difficult hurdles to overcome in becoming financially responsible is getting rid of wrong thinking and concepts of money. With that in mind, it is time for some myth-busting. Listed below are ten common myths about money, followed by the facts that correct the myths. We have even thrown in an extra myth at no charge.

Myth #1: Money is the root of all evil.
Fact: First of all, the scripture is frequently misquoted and taken out of context. Paul writes in 1 Timothy 6:10 (KJV) that "the *love* of money is the root of all evil." He is building a contrast between having a focus on Christ and having a focus on money. Clearly, our focus on Christ is more important. There is also the perspective that would say that "the lack of money is the root of all evil" because it leads to stealing, stress, and strife, none of which are godly.

Myth #2: Money is too complicated for me to understand.
Fact: Ignorance is not bliss when it comes to money. There are two basic means to learn about money, budgeting, investing, etc. The first is to find a mentor or a professional to give some advice and guidelines. Think of it in these terms: If you were going to build an addition to your house, would you ask for advice, and from whom? Your neighbor or someone who has done it before for others? The second way to learn is to make mistakes yourself. Those mistakes could be in both what you did and what you did not do. Learning about money does require a price—you will either pay the price of discipline or the price of regret. When it comes to finances, what you don't know can really hurt you.

Myth #3: It is good to get a tax refund from the government.
Fact: Essentially, you are giving the government a no-interest loan with your money for a year. For instance, if you got a "refund" of

$2400 last year, that means you loaned the government $200 a month interest-free. Then, on April 15, you got your "refund" of $2400. Would you do that for a friend or relative?

Myth #4: The financial pie is finite.
Fact: Many people believe that if they make more, it costs someone else. In reality, the more money you make, the more people you can help. There is an infinite amount of money and an infinite number of ways to make it legally, ethically, and morally. The difference between the haves and the have-nots is usually their perspective about money. Those with money know how to make interest work for them; those without money pay interest.

Myth #5: Investing is risky and I might lose everything.
Fact: The most risky thing about investing is the investor. It is a bigger risk to do nothing than to do something. There is a law of human destiny called the law of cause and effect. This law is simple yet powerful. It states that there is a specific effect for every cause or action. On a macro level this law says that success is *not* an accident. Financial success is the result of doing certain specific actions over and over until you achieve your financial goals.

Myth #6: A good job is all you need.
Fact: Our society has gone from an industrial base to a technology base. There are no lifetime employment opportunities anymore, and without that, we no longer have companies that will take care of our retirement. We are now responsible for our own retirement.

Myth #7: I've never had any money, I never will, so why learn?
Fact: There is a *big* difference between being broke and being poor. Being broke is a temporary financial situation; being poor is an emotional state.

Myth #8: Money can't buy happiness.
Fact: True, but neither can poverty. Additionally, poverty can't pay for a new church building, your children's education, your retirement, or your expenses.

Myth #9: I've got no time to manage my money (or) I'm too busy working to make money.
Fact: Why work if you can't enjoy the fruits of your labor? Is it good stewardship to fritter your money away by not managing it well?

Myth #10: It is not acceptable to talk about money in polite company.
Fact: There are no dumb questions when it comes to money. If you don't ask questions, you are destined to continue down the same road. As we said before, the only difference between a rut and a grave is the depth of the hole and the length of the stay.

Myth #11: It is too early. It is too late. I just had a baby. My kids are in college. My gerbil just died.
Fact: It is *never* the perfect time to start saving. It is an act of discipline that should start *today*.

CHAPTER SEVEN

THE PRINCIPLE OF TITHING

Tithing is fundamental to any God-centered approach to financial management. We have already touched on the importance of tithing, particularly in chapter four, but we want to return to the subject in greater depth because it is such a foundational principle. It is unfortunate that in our day so many Christians give tithing a low priority in their lives and financial thinking. For some, tithing doesn't even enter the picture. "We can barely make ends meet as it is; how can God expect us to tithe?" Others tithe "when we can"—in other words, "when we have enough left over after paying everything else." When money gets tight, they find it very easy to "borrow" or withhold the tithe, saying, "God will understand."

Both of these attitudes suffer from a grossly inadequate understanding of both the nature of tithing and its importance. The first group says, "We can't afford to tithe." If they truly understood tithing, they would know that in reality, they can't afford *not* to tithe. As for the second group, tithing "when we can" is not tithing. Tithing is a commitment, a deliberate decision of the mind and will, not an on-again, off-again activity. Ten percent paid to God after paying everything else is not a true tithe either. A true tithe is setting aside the *first* ten percent for God as an act of faith and in recognition that He is the owner of all.

Some Christians counter that tithing is not a requirement for believers because Jesus never commands us to tithe. While it is true that tithing is an Old Testament concept that is not *explicitly* taught in the New Testament, it is implied. For example, in much of His speech as recorded in the gospels, Jesus assumes that His listeners—whether the common people, His disciples, or the Pharisees and other religious leaders—tithe regularly and will continue to do so. Tithing was a standard part of Jewish life. If anything, the New Testament takes tithing one step further in its emphasis that everything we have belongs to God. We owe Him our total allegiance in every area of life. This idea of total commitment raises the concept of tithing to a whole new level.

Reserving the Firstfruits

The principle of setting aside a portion for God is illustrated many times throughout the Old Testament. Tithing is a very ancient concept, predating the Bible itself, although not the people of the Bible. The very first mention of tithing in Scripture occurs in the fourteenth chapter of Genesis:

> *Then Melchizedek king of Salem brought out bread and wine. He was priest of God Most High, and he blessed Abram, saying, "Blessed be Abram by God Most High, Creator of heaven and earth. And blessed be God Most High, who delivered your enemies into your hand." Then Abram gave him a tenth of everything.* Genesis 14:18-20

Abram gave a tithe to Melchizedek, "priest of God Most High," as an offering to God in recognition of his victory against enemies. An alliance of four kings had invaded the land and attacked and looted several cities, including Sodom, where Abram's nephew, Lot, was living. As the raiders departed, they took Lot with them along with all his possessions. Upon hearing the news, Abram immediately took a band of trained men from his own household and went in pursuit. God gave him victory. Abram rescued Lot and his household and brought them home. Abram's offering of a tithe of the plunder he took in battle was his way of acknowledging God's hand in his victory.

After the Israelites left Egypt under Moses and received the Law from God in the desert of Sinai, the tithe was established as an ongoing practice of setting aside for God the firstfruits—the first tenth of the people's bounty—as a continual reminder that He was the source of everything they had. Reserving the firstfruits was not always an easy lesson to learn, and violating it brought severe consequences, as the Israelites learned to their regret.

After forty years in the wilderness, Israel was ready to enter the Promised Land under the leadership of Joshua. They would have to cross the Jordan River and defeat and displace the inhabitants of the land in order to claim it for themselves and settle it. Their first target after crossing the river was the city of Jericho. God gave explicit instructions as to how they were to proceed, including how to handle the plunder. Once a day for six days the people marched around the walled city in complete silence. On the seventh day they marched around Jericho seven times, again remaining silent. Then Joshua spoke to the people:

> *The seventh time around, when the priests sounded the trumpet blast, Joshua commanded the people, "Shout! For the LORD has given you the city! The city and all that is in it are to be devoted to the LORD. Only Rahab the prostitute and all who are with her in her house shall be spared, because she hid the spies we sent. But keep away from the devoted things, so that you will not bring about your own destruction by taking any of them. Otherwise you will make the camp of Israel liable to destruction and bring trouble on it. All the silver and gold and the articles of bronze and iron are sacred to the LORD and must go into his treasury." When the trumpets sounded, the people shouted, and at the sound of the trumpet, when the people gave a loud shout, the wall collapsed; so every man charged straight in, and they took the city. They devoted the city to the LORD and destroyed with the sword every living thing in it—men and women, young and old, cattle, sheep and donkeys…Then they burned the whole city and everything in it, but they put the silver and gold and the articles of bronze and iron into the treasury of the LORD's house.*
> Joshua 6:16-21, 24

By God's command, Joshua placed the city of Jericho "under the ban," which meant that *everything* in the city was devoted to God. The people were to destroy every living thing and place *all* of the spoils in the treasury of the Lord's house. They were to keep *nothing* back for themselves.

Jericho was a type of tithe, even though the Israelites had to devote one hundred percent to God. God had already told them, "You are going to go into Canaan, and you can take possession of everything that is there. You will eat from vineyards that you did not plant. You will live in homes that you did not build. You are going to enjoy milk and honey. You are going to enjoy wealth. You are going to enjoy it all. You will live on the mountains; you will live in the valleys. It is a beautiful place, much better than Egypt. You will eat the produce of your own hands, much better than manna. Everything in the land is yours. However, when you cross the Jordan and I give the city of Jericho into your hand, everything in that city is Mine. Set it aside as a firstfruits offering to Me. When the city falls, you will find gold and silver and all sorts of treasures. Leave them alone. Do not touch them or take them for yourself. They are to be devoted entirely to Me."

After Jericho, whenever the Israelites captured a city, they were free to divide the spoils among themselves. Only at Jericho—the *first*—were they commanded to give the spoils to the Lord. This was a visual, material lesson in the principle of tithing, of setting aside the first tenth, the firstfruits, as an offering to God.

Everything seemed to go well—at first. Jericho fell, the Israelites destroyed the city, placed its spoils in the treasury, and went on to the next city, Ai. Smaller and weaker than Jericho, Ai seemed a pushover, so Joshua sent only a small force against it. This time, however, the Israelites lost. The men of Ai defeated them, killing thirty-six of them in the process. What had happened? If God was with them, why had they been defeated? Joshua and the other leaders fell on their faces and sought the Lord.

God's answer must have shocked Joshua.

> The LORD said to Joshua, "Stand up! What are you doing down on your face? Israel has sinned; they have violated my covenant, which I commanded them to keep. They have taken some of the devoted things; they have stolen, they have lied, they have put them with their own possessions. That is why the Israelites cannot stand against their enemies; they turn their backs and run because they have been made liable to destruction. I will not be with you anymore unless you destroy whatever among you is devoted to destruction. Go, consecrate the people. Tell

them, 'Consecrate yourselves in preparation for tomorrow; for this is what the LORD, the God of Israel, says: That which is devoted is among you, O Israel. You cannot stand against your enemies until you remove it.'" Joshua 7:10-13

Unknown to Joshua and the rest of the Israelites, one among them, a man named Achan, had violated the ban regarding the devoted items from Jericho: "But the Israelites acted unfaithfully in regard to the devoted things; Achan son of Carmi, the son of Zimri, the son of Zerah, of the tribe of Judah, took some of them. So the LORD's anger burned against Israel" (Joshua 7:1).

Notice how seriously God takes the sin of touching what is devoted to Him: The sin of one man brought guilt upon the whole community. One man disobeyed and everybody paid; thirty-six even paid with their lives in the abortive attack on Ai, even though they did not participate in Achan's sin.

In the verses that follow, God directs a process in which Achan is exposed as the guilty party. After confessing to stealing a beautiful robe, a cache of silver coins, and a wedge of gold, Achan and his entire family (who apparently had conspired in the sin or at least in its cover-up) were stoned to death and their belongings burned. That's how important it was for the Israelites to purge the evil in their midst.

Here is the principle of tithing: *The firstfruit, the tithe, is reserved for the Lord.* We are to set it aside for Him and not use it for any other purpose. Properly, the tithe comes off the top—the *first* ten percent of our income—which is why it is called a "firstfruits offering." For the Jews, the tithe involved more than just money. They tithed the first harvest of their crops, the first lamb or goat born each year, the first profit from their work; in short, they brought a tithe of every bounty they received from God.

Tithing is the first battle we must win on our way to financial stability and good stewardship. Until we get our hearts and our practices right about the tithe, nothing else will work as it should. Israel was unable to proceed in their conquest of Canaan until they dealt with Achan's sin of touching what was devoted to the Lord. After they took action, the Lord blessed them once again and they proceeded to conquer the land.

There is a lesson here for us. Too often we are like Achan, touching the things reserved for God, and then wondering why we are not experiencing victory, why every day is a financial struggle. God says, "Set aside the tithe for Me, and I will give you the rest." Heaven's economy is different from ours. By observation, we've seen that people who are faithful tithers can do more with their remaining ninety percent than other people can do who keep one hundred percent for themselves. God can do more with our ten-percent tithe than any of us could ever do with our ninety percent. There is no way to explain this in logical, human terms. God's math may not "add up" on earth, but it works.

Robbing God

The Bible also describes disregarding the tithe as robbing God. How do you rob God? How do you rob someone who owns everything and possesses infinite resources? That's a good question, yet that is exactly what the Lord Himself said we do every time we fail to tithe. Furthermore, our failure to tithe is a direct cause of our failure to receive God's blessings in our lives. Listen to what the Lord says in Malachi:

> *"I the LORD do not change. So you, O descendants of Jacob, are not destroyed. Ever since the time of your forefathers you have turned away from my decrees and have not kept them. Return to me, and I will return to you, says the LORD Almighty. But you ask, How are we to return? Will a man rob God? Yet you rob me. But you ask, "How do we rob you?" In tithes and offerings. You are under a curse—the whole nation of you—because you are robbing me. Bring the whole tithe into the storehouse, that there may be food in my house. Test me in this, says the LORD Almighty, and see if I will not throw open the floodgates of heaven and pour out so much blessing that you will not have room enough for it."* Malachi 3:6-10

The Lord says that the entire nation was under a curse because some were not paying their tithes. That sounds a lot like the case with Achan, where his sin brought a curse on all the people. It is the same principle. Failure to tithe causes God to withhold His blessings. This is just as true today as it was in Old Testament times. There is no way that we can be fully blessed by God if we do not tithe. Going a step further, if we do not tithe, any church we are a part of will miss out on part of God's blessing. Why? Just take a look at Israel. When one person sinned, the entire community suffered; when one person was blessed, everybody benefited.

Think of it this way. As Christians, we are part of a spiritual family, and we belong to a local community of believers called the church. God blesses us so that we can bless others. That means that we are supposed to share our blessings with those in our community. If we miss out on some of our blessings through our failure to tithe, then others in our community miss out on those blessings that we otherwise would have shared with them. American Christians get caught up too easily in the Lone Ranger syndrome, assuming that our walk with God and the decisions we make in that walk are essentially private matters that affect no one but ourselves. Sometimes we forget the corporate, community element of our faith. We are responsible for our decisions not only to God but also to the local community of believers of which we are a part. If Achan had remembered that, he would have spared himself and Israel a whole lot of grief.

In our church, every member is encouraged to tithe for his or her own spiritual benefit as well as that of the church. We take tithing very seriously. Only committed tithers can serve in any leadership position in our church. We take the view that individuals who are not personally investing in the work of the Kingdom of God do not have the right to make decisions on how to spend the church's money.

Still, the question remains, how does failing to tithe rob God? Part of it is attitude. When we do not tithe, we make a statement that God and His expectations are not very important to us. As far as attitude is concerned, there is no fundamental difference between failing to pay God's tithe and failing to pay the rent or the electric bill. Failure to pay legitimate creditors is a form of stealing.

Malachi 3:10 gives us a clue to another way that we rob God when we do not tithe: "'Bring the whole tithe into the storehouse, that there may be food in my house. Test me in this,' says the LORD Almighty, 'and see if I will not throw open the floodgates of heaven and pour out so much blessing that you will not have room enough for it.'" This verse is the one place in Scripture where God specifically tells us to test Him. It is as though He is saying, "Bring your tithe, your *whole* tithe, to Me; let Me *prove* myself to you as One who can shower you with overwhelming blessing." Can you imagine the Creator of the universe, the Lord of Heaven and earth, asking us to let Him prove Himself? That shows just how much God wants us to be in right relationship with Him.

God promises that if we will be faithful with the tithe, He will open the floodgates of Heaven and pour out more blessing than we can handle. Notice that He says "blessing"—singular—rather than the plural "blessings." Even just one of God's blessings is enough to overwhelm us. Have you ever been blessed that way? Through the years, God has blessed us both many times and we're not ashamed to admit it. Sometimes when people get blessed they are ashamed to say anything, out of fear that people will think they are bragging. Of course it's bragging to talk about our blessings! We're bragging on God! We would rather have one of God's blessings than all the blessings the world could ever give.

Although God has blessed us richly, He hasn't yet blessed us so much that we no longer have room for any more. How about you? God says, "I will bless you until you don't have enough room for it." Now we're thinking, "Lord, wait a minute. We know we are living in Your blessing, but there must be something else. We've both got savings accounts, and there's a lot of room left in them. (Ken says his savings account looks like a marble inside of a fifty-gallon barrel.) What do you mean about a blessing so big that we won't have room enough for it?"

One thing should be crystal clear from this verse: *God really wants to bless His people.* He wants to bless us and He wants to do it in a big way. Why doesn't He? According to verse eight, it's because we are robbing God in our tithes and offerings. It's not about the money. Remember, Heaven does not have a cash flow problem. God is not sitting up in Heaven saying, "Oh, my, the Hubbards and the Paganos didn't pay their tithes today. What am I going to do? I guess I'll have to close down the west wing until I get more money." Some pastors have had people say to them, "I don't agree with what you said (or did), so I'm taking my tithe and getting out of here." Our feeling for those types of people is, "Don't let the door hit you on the way out. Your forty dollars a week (or whatever) will not affect the Kingdom of God. In fact, your forty dollars didn't affect the Kingdom even when you were giving it if you were giving it with the wrong attitude." We don't tithe so that we can have a voice. Our dollar doesn't buy us a vote in the church. We tithe because God commanded it, and because we love Him.

If money is not the problem, what is? How do we rob God? Think about your children. If you have no children, then think back to when you were a child. One of the things we parents like to do is bless our kids. Sometimes we say to them something like, "If you clean your room and take out the garbage and wash the dishes, we'll go to the movies." We really want to give our children a good time, but we also have expectations of them. Their blessing—the trip to the movies—is contingent upon their meeting our expectations—clean room, empty garbage can, clean dishes. We have set it up that way.

What happens if they don't do what we ask? First of all, as parents we are disappointed because our children let us down. Second, if we want to be good and effective parents, we must hold to the terms of the agreement. Otherwise, they will think we are liars. Because they failed to do their chores, they (and we) don't go to the movies. Their failure to do what they were supposed to do causes them to miss out on the blessing, and we as the parents miss out on the opportunity and the *joy* of being able to bless them.

That's how we rob God in our tithes and offerings. He is our Father and, like any natural father, wants to bless us, but cannot when we disobey Him and do not follow the principles He has established. We miss out on the blessing, and rob God of the opportunity to bless us. He is a giving God and delights in giving good things to His children. Our disobedience robs Him of that delight, because He can't bless us when we don't do what He says. God wants to bless us, but we have to do it His way. If we do—if we honor Him with the tithe—we untie His hands. We take the kink out of the hose and make it possible for Him to pour out His blessings on us. We make it possible for Him to open the floodgates of Heaven.

The Tithe Is a Seed

In the Kingdom of God there are only two seasons: seedtime and harvest, and they are a continuing cycle. Seeds planted produce a harvest. From the harvest, some is held back as seed for the next seedtime. If we want a harvest, we have to plant seed. If we want a seedtime next season, we have to set back some of the harvest this season. It is a foolish man who gets a bushel of corn and eats it all. He then has no seed with which to grow his next bushel.

We believe that is where we are in America today. Right now, Americans as a whole spend much more than what they save or set back. Far too many of us spend much more than we bring in, and we have the sky-high debt to prove it. Many Americans complain about the state of the economy. One of the biggest problems with our economy is the "credit trap" that allows us to consume more than we pay for. At least, that's the way it appears at first. "Play now, pay later" has a lot of appeal until we realize that in the end what we pay in principal plus interest is much more than the value of what we bought.

This should concern us, because the same thing happens in the Church. God said there would be seedtime and harvest. Without seed, there can be no harvest. How can the Church expect a harvest if we are always spending our seed instead of planting it? This is where tithing comes in. Our tithe is a seed which we plant (or invest) in the Kingdom of Heaven. Seeds invested in Heaven always bring an abundant return, much better than seed invested anywhere else.

God gave us the tithe as a simple principle of taking a seed and putting it back into the soil so it will produce a harvest. Today in America we are too busy chowing down on our bushel of corn to reinvest any seed. We are too busy partying to think about the future. We call friends and neighbors and say, "Come on over; let me show you what I've got." We like to flaunt our money. Even when we don't have money, we try to act like we do. Instead of saving some of our substance for the future, we party on our wealth as if there will be no tomorrow. Perhaps you've seen the bumper sticker that says, "We are spending our grandchildren's inheritance." It's supposed to be a joke, but sadly enough, there is a lot of truth in it.

What is the power of a seed? Some of you may think, "But my seed is so small. I don't make much money anyway. What good could my tithe possibly do?" First of all, remember the principle of multiplication. Each of us by ourselves can do very little. Together, however, we can do a lot. God can take our gifts, our tithes, and multiply them in ways we can't even begin to imagine. His economy operates differently from that of the world. Secondly, remember that the issue is not the *amount* we give but the *attitude* in which we give it.

Jesus made this clear to His disciples one day when they were sitting in the Temple courts:

Jesus sat down opposite the place where the offerings were put and watched the crowd putting their money into the temple treasury. Many rich people threw in large amounts. But a poor widow came and put in two very small copper coins, worth only a fraction of a penny. Calling his disciples to him, Jesus said, "I tell you the truth, this poor widow has put more into the treasury than all the others. They all gave out of their wealth; but she, out of her poverty, put in everything—all she had to live on."

Mark 12:41-44

This widow, by putting into the Temple treasury all the money she had to live on, demonstrated both her love for God and her faith in His ability and promise to care for her needs. What little money she had, she reinvested in God's Kingdom, trusting Him for a harvest in her life. That is the true spirit of tithing.

How powerful is a seed? More powerful than we can imagine. One small seed planted (invested) in the soil can return a harvest that is a hundredfold, a thousandfold, or more. When we tithe, God can use our tithe—whatever the amount—to accomplish His purpose and bring a return far beyond what our money alone could ever accomplish. Because this is God's economy, we cannot always understand how it works; we have to simply trust that it does. The gospel of Mark records two parables of Jesus that illustrate both the power of a seed and the mysterious way that God's economy operates:

"This is what the kingdom of God is like. A man scatters seed on the ground. Night and day, whether he sleeps or gets up, the seed sprouts and grows, though he does not know how. All by itself the soil produces grain—first the stalk, then the head, then the full kernel in the head. As soon as the grain is ripe, he puts the sickle to it, because the harvest has come." Again he said, "What shall we say the kingdom of God is like, or what parable shall we use to describe it? It is like a mustard seed, which is the smallest seed you plant in the ground. Yet when planted, it grows and becomes the largest of all garden plants, with such big branches that the birds of the air can perch in its shade."

Mark 4:26-32

Don't worry if your seed seems small. If what is in your hand is too small to be the harvest, then use it as your seed and plant it. If you are not currently tithing, start now. If you are tithing already, keep on being faithful. If you honor God's principle of tithing, He will honor your obedience. If by your tithing you demonstrate that you recognize His ownership of all you have and you trust in His ability and desire to bless you, He will begin to turn your situation around.

Tithing is an investment in the Kingdom of God and the first step on the journey to solid financial management and good stewardship. If your attitude toward the tithe is correct, your attitude toward the rest of your money and other assets will change. What you once saw as yours you will now recognize as God's, and just as subject to His will and direction as your tithe. Getting right with your ten percent will help you get right with your ninety percent. Learning to acknowledge God as Lord of all your assets will make a difference in how you use your money. Instead of being controlled by your finances, you will control your finances, and therein lies freedom.

CHAPTER EIGHT

THE PRINCIPLE OF INVESTING

Several times in the first half of this book we have mentioned the importance of investing. Investing multiplies our money, while spending only consumes it. Money invested wisely turns a profit, which provides more money that can be invested to turn an even greater profit, which provides even more money that can be invested to turn an even greater profit and so on. In this chapter, we want to examine more closely the biblical principle of investing. Wise and consistent investing is one of the keys to financial freedom.

Financial freedom does not necessarily mean being enormously wealthy with money oozing out of the pores of your body. When we say "financial freedom," we mean being in the place where money serves you rather than you serving it, where you have learned how to make your money work for you, and where you are earning interest instead of paying interest. Essentially, financial freedom means having the financial flexibility to do with your money whatever you want, whenever you want, whenever the need or opportunity arises.

This is not the same as spending your money recklessly on your own lusts and desires. It is instead wise investing and generous giving under the leadership of the Holy Spirit, with proper and due care given to meeting personal needs and expenses. Financial freedom means that when an opportunity arises to plant a financial seed of investment in an overseas missions effort, you will have the money to do so. It means being able to contribute financially to help someone who needs groceries or to have their car repaired. It means having the capacity to bless others as God has blessed you.

Financial freedom comes from learning how to use our money and other financial resources to turn a profit. We believe that God has commanded us to turn a profit and holds us accountable accordingly. Remember that fruitfulness and multiplication are fundamental to God's purpose for our lives. God has given us the ability to produce wealth, and He never gives anything without a reason. Why would He give us the ability to produce wealth unless He wants us to produce wealth?

Producing wealth is another way of saying "turning a profit." A profit is how much you have left when the transaction is over. Many people fail to turn a profit in their personal finances because they are more concerned about *making* money than they are about *keeping* it. Where profitability is concerned, the issue is not how much money we make, but how much money we keep. Turning a profit has nothing to do with an amount. Even though it does take money to make money, it does not take much money to make money. We can turn a profit at *any* income level. The key is learning and following the principle of investing.

God wants to bless us, but He also wants us to turn a profit. One reason so many of us miss out on the financial blessings of God in our lives is because we spend our income on liabilities rather than on assets. We will never turn a profit until we start investing. Another way to describe investing is putting our money to work. There is more than one way to make money. God said that He gave us the ability to produce wealth; He never said He would just *give* us wealth. If we will learn to follow His principles, then that seed of wealth-producing ability inside us will begin to bear fruit. The ability is there, but we have to work it.

The principle of investing and turning a profit is so important that Jesus told a parable that directly addresses the subject. It is recorded in the twenty-fifth chapter of the gospel of Matthew. Matthew, you remember, was a tax collector, a man who certainly knew a few things about money! Luke records a somewhat different version of the same basic story, which Jesus told at the house of Zacchaeus, another tax collector. Even though this parable, like all the others, has a spiritual lesson at heart, its application to stewardship and financial management is too plain to miss. Commonly known as the parable of the talents, it could just as easily be called the parable of the three investors.

God Invests in Each of Us

In Matthew's gospel, the parable of the three investors occurs in the context of the teaching Jesus gave on the Mount of Olives concerning signs and events related to the end-times. Most of chapter 24 is devoted to a description of the signs of Jesus' coming and of the end of the age (Matthew 24:3). Jesus follows this teaching with a series of three parables to drive home the importance of being prepared for His return. The story of the three investors is the third of these parables. Rounding out the entire lesson is Jesus' description of the judgment of "the sheep and the goats."

Spiritually speaking, the parable of the three investors is about being faithful *now* in expectation of Christ's return. We can easily make a financial application to the story because good stewardship is an important part of both being faithful and being prepared. Two of the three investors understood this; the third investor, unfortunately, did not. Let's look more closely now and see what Jesus had to say about investing.

> *"Again, it* (the Kingdom of Heaven) *will be like a man going on a journey, who called his servants and entrusted his property to them. To one he gave five talents of money, to another two talents, and to another one talent, each according to his ability. Then he went on his journey."* Matthew 25:14-15

Today, a talent would be roughly the equivalent of a thousand dollars in our currency. This man entrusted eight thousand dollars to his three servants. He gave one of them five thousand, another received two thousand, and the third was given one thousand. That doesn't sound fair, does it? Why didn't he give them all the same amount? This man knew his servants well; he gave to each of them "according to his ability." He placed no burden of responsibility or expectation on any of his servants that he knew they were incapable of. It had nothing to do with fairness but everything to do with ability. Besides, it would have been truly unfair to give five talents to the third servant, knowing that it was more than he could handle. By investing in each servant according to his ability, this man was being eminently fair.

113

Any wise investor will watch out for two things: first, he will be careful not to put all of his eggs in one basket, and second, he will be careful not to put more eggs in one basket than will bring a return. God is the same way. He invests in each of us according to our ability and our demonstrated faithfulness. If we have "five-talent" ability, He will invest five talents in us; "two-talent" ability will receive two; and "one-talent" ability, one. It is all proportional. God has our very best interests at heart, so He does not place on us more than we can handle. However, He *does* expect us to handle well what He *has* placed on us. God invests in each of us, and He is deeply interested in what we do with that investment.

Remember that God invests in the stock market. He invests most heavily where He will receive the greatest return. If we prove faithful in small things, He will trust us with bigger things. The investments we receive from God are usually in seed form; it is our responsibility to bring them to maturity. If we ask for a tree, God will give us an acorn and say, "Get to it." If we ask for a job making $80,000 a year, He may put us in one that starts at $40,000 a year.

The Scripture does not mention this, but we suspect that the servant who received five talents had once been a "one-talent" man. Through wise management of small amounts, he had earned the trust of his master in managing larger portions. If we are to increase our wealth, we must increase our ability to make wealth. As we have said before, it is a matter of attitude, not amount. Even millionaires go broke sometimes, but they rarely stay broke because they know how to make money. That is what made them millionaires to begin with.

Take a look at your own situation. Remember, you can change your situation if you change. What you have today is not all you can have or, necessarily, all you will have. God won't trust you with five talents until you prove you can handle two. He won't trust you with two until you prove you can handle one. Faithful management with a little will lead to God trusting you with more. That is a clear biblical principle and you can (excuse the pun) "take it to the bank."

We Should Reinvest Right Away

Having entrusted his three servants with his property, the man left on a long journey. What happened next reveals what each servant thought about himself, his master, his master's money, and his own responsibility.

> *The man who had received the five talents went at once and put his money to work and gained five more. So also, the one with the two talents gained two more. But the man who had received the one talent went off, dug a hole in the ground and hid his master's money.*   Matthew 25:16-18

Notice what the first servant did: He went *at once* and put his five talents to work. I like that. This is the guy who had the most ability, and he knew just what to do. Wasting no time, he invested his money and received double in return. It's not important how he did it; what's important is that he had the knowledge necessary to do it. The second servant did the same thing: He invested his two talents and also received a double return. So it is not a matter of *amount*, but of *attitude* and *knowledge*. Knowledge affects our attitude because it gives us the confidence we need to take action. What good is it to have a million dollars to invest if you are too scared of losing it to do anything with it? Investing is always risky, but wise investing takes risks based on knowledge.

The actions of the first two servants illustrate an important principle about investing: *Start now.* Don't delay, because the longer you delay, the less likely you are to do anything at all. This doesn't mean you should be careless or reckless in your investments, but it does mean you should not waste time, because time is money. Start small, start big, but *start!* "But I don't have any money to invest." That's probably not true. Every one of us, no matter how tight our money may seem, has some "fat" somewhere that we can trim. Take a close look at your financial situation. Somewhere you probably have a few dollars you can shake loose on a regular basis to invest, even if it is just $5.00 a week. Buy one less case of soda this week or rent one less DVD and invest the money instead. Put it in a savings account if nothing else.

Do you want a new financial beginning? Then start today. Somewhere, somehow, find out a way to invest with what you already have. Talk to a financial professional or a trusted friend who has investment experience. Check out *The Wall Street Journal* and other financial publications for tips on investing. Read books. Ask questions. The answers are out there if you know where to look. Even if you *don't* know where to look, there are people who can help you there, as well. Visit your local library; someone there should be able to steer you in the right direction. The only one who can hold you back is *you.*

We are assuming at this point that you are already investing spiritually—that you have paid God with your tithe. If not, that's where you should begin. Next, make sure you have paid Uncle Sam. (Actually, Uncle Sam is pretty good about making sure he gets his cut!) Third, pay yourself. I don't mean just pay your bills and other expenses. Do that, certainly, but pay yourself something extra, something you can invest to build for the future.

The first two servants put their money to work. By investing wisely, they doubled their money. This is a secret that all financially successful people know: *Put your money to work.* There is more than one way to make more money. You can work longer hours, taking time away from your family and the things you would really like to do. Some people work two or even three jobs. The other alternative is to take a portion of your money and let it go to work for you. If you invest wisely, your money can be making money while you spend time walking in the park with your spouse or fishing with your son or dating your daughter. Some people work so hard making money that they never have time to enjoy the fruits of their labor. That doesn't make any sense.

By all appearances, the third servant did not understand any of this. He apparently had no concept of the power of investing; perhaps he simply didn't care. At any rate, his response to receiving his talent was very different from that of his two fellow servants. Instead of investing his money or even putting it into the bank to earn interest, he simply buried it.

During and after the Great Depression, when so many financial institutions failed, taking customers' savings with them, there were many people who did not trust banks. For a long time it was a common practice to take your money, place it in a Folger's coffee can or some other durable container, and bury it in the backyard. That might prevent you from losing your money, but it will never grow that way, either. That is just what the third servant did. He buried his money and forgot about it.

Turn a Profit

The rich man in Jesus' parable was gone for a long time before he returned to settle accounts with them. This too suggests a key factor in investing: *patience*. Investing will turn a profit, but it takes time. Don't invest $20.00 today and expect to have $10,000 next month. Successful investors invest for the long haul, thinking ahead to the future rather than focusing on short-term gain. This is a tough concept for most Americans. After all, we live in the now, we work hard in the now and we want the rewards—*now*. Too often we are unwilling to wait. Instead of holding out for the best, we settle for second-best.

Another problem many of us have is the get-rich-quick syndrome. We dream of receiving sudden wealth with no effort on our part, whether through an inheritance, winning the sweepstakes or the lottery, or by some other unexpected windfall. We want the palace without the pit; the suite without the sweat. There are no legitimate get-rich-quick schemes. We've all heard it said, "If something sounds too good to be true, it probably is." In life, as well as in the business and finance worlds, there really is no such thing as a free lunch.

God has invested in each of us and expects us to bring Him a return. He does not want us to sit idly by and do nothing—like the third investor did. At the same time, He does not want us to be reckless, treating our investments as though we were at the gambling table, risking everything on one throw of the dice. Instead, God is looking for us to display wisdom, discernment, patience, and good judgment. We are, after all, stewards of *His* resources, not owners. Eventually, a day of reckoning will come when we will reap the rewards—or the consequences—of our stewardship. This is exactly what happened to the three investors.

> *"After a long time the master of those servants returned and settled accounts with them. The man who had received the five talents brought the other five. 'Master,' he said, 'you entrusted me with five talents. See, I have gained five more.' His master replied, 'Well done, good and faithful servant! You have been faithful with a few things; I will put you in charge of many things. Come and share your master's happiness!' The man with the two talents also came. 'Master,' he said, 'you entrusted me with two talents; see, I have gained two more.' His master replied,*

> *'Well done, good and faithful servant! You have been faithful*
> *with a few things; I will put you in charge of many things. Come*
> *and share your master's happiness!'* "   Matthew 25:19-23

Receiving double on your investment is always a good return, no matter what the amount. No wonder the master in this story was so pleased with the first two investors and so willing to trust them with more of his money. They had proven their faithfulness, their ability, and their worth. Because they returned double on their investment, the master put them in charge of twice as much as they had before. Listen, if we gave you five thousand dollars of our money and sometime later you returned it along with another five thousand you had made with it, don't you think we would be willing to trust you with that ten thousand and say, "Go do it again, friend"?

Some of you may be thinking, "But Jesus really wasn't talking about money in this parable. He was talking about our faithfulness in living the Christian life and getting ready for His return." That is certainly true, but as we said before, the principle of investing can apply to money also, because every area of our lives, including our finances, is of great interest to God. While not neglecting the spiritual meaning, we need to be careful not to overspiritualize, either. The point is that God will invest more in us if we prove faithful with what we already have. Talking money again, if God knows that He can trust you with a ten-thousand-dollar raise this year—if He knows that you will increase your tithe to reflect your new income, add to your missionary support, increase your giving to the building fund, etc.—He will give it to you. Then you will have an opportunity to take some of that ten-thousand-dollar increase and put that money to work for you.

Here is the bottom line: God invests in us because He wants us to turn a profit. No matter where we may be financially, we don't have to get more money before we can turn a profit. Because He has given us the ability to produce wealth, we should be able to turn a profit at any level. If your financial situation is not working with what you're doing, you need to change what you're doing. You will never get to the next level until you fix the level you are on. Here is the good news, though: If you can fix your finances at *this* level, you will be able to fix them at *any* level. Bring your financial practices into line with God's principle of investing and you *will* turn a profit—every time. Guaranteed.

You Can't Reap What You Don't Sow

If Jesus' story ended there, everything would be fine. The first two investors have proven themselves profitable, have been entrusted with more, and have been invited to share their master's happiness. Unfortunately, we must still consider the third investor, and his day of reckoning. Notice how, the moment he comes into his master's presence, he starts making excuses.

> *"Then the man who had received the one talent came. 'Master,' he said, 'I knew that you are a hard man, harvesting where you have not sown and gathering where you have not scattered seed. So I was afraid and went out and hid your talent in the ground. See, here is what belongs to you.' His master replied, 'You wicked, lazy servant! So you knew that I harvest where I have not sown and gather where I have not scattered seed? Well then, you should have put my money on deposit with the bankers, so that when I returned I would have received it back with interest. Take the talent from him and give it to the one who has the ten talents. For everyone who has will be given more, and he will have an abundance. Whoever does not have, even what he has will be taken from him. And throw that worthless servant outside, into the darkness, where there will be weeping and gnashing of teeth.'"*
>
> Matthew 25:24-30

How's this for brass—not only does the investor make excuses for not turning a profit; he even implies that it is his master's fault! "I'm sorry, sir, but I didn't produce because you are a hard man and you scared me." Was the master "hard" because he expected a fair and honest return on his investment? Was he "hard" because he challenged his investor to rise to his potential? Was he "hard" because he hoped this investor would prove his worth and receive the opportunity to rise to greater things as did the two investors before him?

Haven't we all been guilty of the same thing? At one time or another, haven't we all played the blame game? "Well, my boss just doesn't like me." "I was born on the wrong side of the tracks." "I didn't learn about all this." Making excuses won't change a thing. We can blame everybody else as long as we want to, but it won't help. "My boss doesn't pay me enough." Then find another job. It's probably not really your boss's fault anyway. Even if he doesn't pay you enough, that's still no excuse. Successful investing and turning a profit do not depend on how much you make but on how you use what you make. Besides, you agreed to work for that amount of money when you took the job, so don't complain. This is reminiscent of the guy who thought he wasn't making enough and went to see his boss. "Boss," he said confidently, "I really think you ought to pay me what I'm worth around here." His boss looked at him and replied, "John, I'd love to pay you what you're worth, but there *is* a minimum wage law."

The truth is, you cannot reap what you have not sown. You will receive no return for an investment you do not make. Some folks say, "Someday my ship will come in." It won't if you never send it out. Financial insufficiency feeds a welfare mindset, a poverty mindset that says, "The world owes me a living." Many people go through life that way, getting by on handouts and on the generosity of others. Genuine need is one thing; a life of dependency is something else altogether. If you have no money and no prospects of getting any, what good will it do for me to pay your rent? What will you do next month? We must learn to sow seeds and invest for ourselves, and teach others to do the same. There is an old Chinese proverb that says, "Give a man a fish and you feed him for a day; teach a man to fish and you feed him for a lifetime." Give a man a fish one day and he will come back for another the next. Teach him to fish…a lifetime of eating because of one fishing lesson. That's quite a return on a small investment!

There is another side to sowing and reaping. The investor said to his master, "I knew that you are a hard man, harvesting where you have not sown and gathering where you have not scattered seed." These words contain a great principle. All through this book we have said we have to plant seeds if we want to reap a harvest, and that is true. Nevertheless, we believe it is equally true that when we come under God's favor, we can harvest where we have not sown and gather where we have not scattered seed. For example, sometimes we preach and people get saved in our church for whom others have been praying for years. Momma or Daddy or Grandma has been sowing seeds of prayer every day for years, but we reap the harvest of seeing that person come to Christ. There may be other times when someone will come into our church and write a check in support of a ministry that they have never personally been fed by. They see a ministry that is reaching people and fulfilling the Great Commission, and they want to contribute even in a small way. We reap a harvest from their life even though we never sowed a seed there.

Excuses or no excuses, the third investor's failure to invest his talent drew a sharp rebuke from his master. The investor brought back what was given to him and returned it intact. Not a single penny was missing. That earned him a rebuke? If he had brought only part of it back and said, "Sorry, but I needed a new robe and sandals, and last week I had to repair the roof of my house," that would be worthy of the master's anger. That's beside the point. The investor received a rebuke because he failed to meet his master's expectations. His master did not give his talent for it to be buried in the ground but to be invested so it could multiply. The investor failed in his responsibility. He failed to turn a profit—in fact, he didn't even try—and thus earned a rebuke.

Three Profit-Killers

Why did the third investor respond so differently from the other two? Verses 25-30 reveal at least three things about his temperament and character that help explain his behavior. These three factors, or character flaws, will kill profit-making in our lives every time just as they did for this man.

First, he was *afraid*. Fear paralyzes faith. First cousin to fear is greed. Fear and greed are the only reasons we don't invest. They are also the top reasons why we do not tithe. We want to live for the moment, not for the future. "I'm afraid of losing my money." "I'm afraid that if I play the stock market, I'll mess up because I won't know what I'm doing." "What if I give extra money for that, and then can't do this?"

We cannot allow fear to paralyze our faith and kill our ability to turn a profit. Faith is the bridge by which we reach everything we hope for. As long as fear keeps us off the bridge, we will never reach our goals or our destiny.

Secondly, this third investor was *lazy*. When he returned the talent he had hidden in the ground, his master said, "You wicked, lazy servant!" So not only was he afraid; he was lazy as well. Fear and laziness—either one alone will kill profit, but together they make fruitfulness all but impossible. God will not bless lazy people; it's that simple.

Over and over again the Bible warns against laziness:

Go to the ant, you sluggard; consider its ways and be wise! It has no commander, no overseer or ruler, yet it stores its provisions in summer and gathers its food at harvest. How long will you lie there, you sluggard? When will you get up from your sleep? A little sleep, a little slumber, a little folding of the hands to rest— and poverty will come on you like a bandit and scarcity like an armed man. Proverbs 6:6-11

Lazy hands make a man poor, but diligent hands bring wealth. Proverbs 10:4

A sluggard does not plow in season; so at harvest time he looks but finds nothing. Proverbs 20:4

For even when we were with you, we gave you this rule: "If a man will not work, he shall not eat." We hear that some among you are idle. They are not busy; they are busybodies. Such people we command and urge in the Lord Jesus Christ to settle down and earn the bread they eat. 2 Thessalonians 3:10-12

Thirdly, this third investor was *stupid* in the literal sense, because he knew better. Being stupid is when you know better but go ahead anyway. How can we tell that he knew better? He knew his master was coming back and would require an accounting, yet he did nothing. He should have done *something*. If he was afraid about what to do, he could have followed the other two investors to see what they did. He could have found someone else who was already successful in investing and learned from that person. He simply had no excuse for doing nothing.

Neither do we. God has given us the ability to produce wealth and desires us to turn a profit. He wants us to make the most of our lives in every arena, including the financial. Nothing delights Him more than to see His children fulfill their potential. Learn the principle of investing and start today.

When we were both growing up, we were never taught about finances. Our families never thought much about the future; we were too busy trying to get by day by day. We're not ashamed of where we came from, but knowing what we know now, we would be ashamed to stay there.

I (Ken) once said to the Lord, "If I'm going to do the things that You've called me to do, I've got to be able to produce wealth better than I'm doing." I didn't know how, so I started looking for godly people who were doing well financially. Their financial strength was not because they had multimillion-dollar jobs but that they were good stewards of what God had given them. I started hanging around them, asking questions, and doing what they did. I learned a lot, which is why I recommend the same thing for you. If you don't know what to do, just follow someone else's lead. Learn to invest, and do it consistently. Then, the promise of Matthew 25:29a will be for you, too: "For everyone who has will be given more, and he will have an abundance."

CHAPTER NINE

THE PRINCIPLE OF DEBT-FREE LIVING

As a general rule, Americans are saddled with debt. More and more we mortgage our future to satisfy our greed and lust of the present. With credit so readily available for most of us, the discipline of delayed reward has become a thing of the past. Debt is so prevalent that many people assume it is the normal way of life. We recognize that sometimes in some cases debt is unavoidable. Something is wrong, however, when indebtedness becomes a lifestyle. Indebtedness eats away at our assets, robs us of our dreams, and can push us to the very brink of financial ruin. It is a trap so subtle and so common that it can ensnare us before we know what is happening.

Let us illustrate the effect of indebtedness by using the example of coal miners who worked for the big coal companies in the ninteenth and early twentieth centuries. There is an old folk song called "Sixteen Tons" that talks about the life of the coal miner. At one point the song says, "Saint Peter, don't you call me, 'cause I can't go; I owe my soul to the company store." In those early days before modern labor laws and civil rights and workers' rights legislation, miners employed by the big mining companies usually lived with their families on company property in company-owned houses. They received their pay not in regular money but in company-issued scrip that they could use at the company-owned store to buy groceries, clothing, and other goods that they needed. Outside the company store, the scrip was useless because it was not legal tender.

More often than not, the miners' wages did not match up with the prices of items in the company store, so they would have to borrow against their future wages in order to buy what they needed at the moment. In no time at all, most of them were so in debt that it seemed like they had indeed "sold their souls" to the company store. They could not quit or leave as long as they owed the company, and all they had was company scrip, which they could not use anywhere else. With no way to make money elsewhere, they were trapped in an escalating cycle of debt. Their "employment" as miners became a form of legalized bondage.

That's how debt can trap us. Credit makes it so easy for us to live beyond our means—for a time. Eventually, however, reality catches up but our checkbooks don't. We can never get ahead, because we have to constantly use tomorrow's resources to pay for today's excesses. Debt is a trap that we need to get out of and learn to avoid in the future. But how? In this chapter, we want to look at several practical steps for getting out of debt and getting onto the road to debt-free living.

Get God

How do we get out of debt? Number one, *get God*. You might say, "Well, I've got God, and I'm so far in debt I can't keep my head above water." Get God involved in your *money*. We gladly involve God in other areas of our lives—parenting, relationships, health needs, church— but for some reason regard money as a different matter. Is God involved in your grocery shopping, in your Christmas shopping? Do you take Him with you to the mall? Do you seek His guidance before a purchase? When you and your spouse sit down to talk money and plan your household budget, do you invite God to sit at the table with you to show you what to do? How important is God's will to you when making your financial decisions?

If you think that sounds radical, well, getting out of debt often takes a radical solution. If you are in debt up to your eyeballs and the water is still rising, you'd better do something pretty quick. Obviously, something is out of whack. Something has to change. Nothing will change as long as you insist on doing things the way you have been doing them. Remember the definition of insanity: doing things the same way over and over and expecting different results. There are people who sit around saying, "One day I'm going to be out of debt. I can't wait; it's going to be great." They are not making any more money this year than last year but are spending more, they still don't have any money in savings, and they still keep their credit cards maxed out, but they're *going to get out of debt!* That's crazy. It'll never happen. Not in this lifetime, anyway.

Some of us seem to live in a fantasy world when it comes to dealing with our debts. It's almost as though we expect our fairy godmother to appear, wave a magic wand over our checkbook, and make all our bills go away. God is no fairy godmother. He *can* work miracles, but He's not going to come in and take our bills and loan payments and simply erase them. If we get Him involved—if we turn our finances over to Him—He will work *with* us to get out of debt. He has already shown us over and over in His Word how to be good stewards. We need to apply those biblical principles to our own situation.

For many of us, the root of the problem comes right back down to the issue of whose money it is. We may say with our lips that our money belongs to God—ten percent of it, anyway—but our actions say otherwise. Many Christians stumble over the issue of the tithe; even more trip up when it comes to the other ninety percent. Why are we so reluctant to get God involved with our money? Are we ashamed of the way we are using it? Are we afraid He will tell us to stop buying some of the things we are buying? Are we afraid of the changes we know He will want us to make? Or could it be that we simply are not convinced that He is interested in our financial affairs?

Psalm 24:1 says, "The earth is the LORD's, and everything in it, the world, and all who live in it." Since everything belongs to God, why *wouldn't* He be interested in our money and how we use it? Some folks say, "You don't need to talk about money. Don't worry about it. God will meet your needs." Yes, He will, as long as we act responsibly. How can God meet our needs if we run off and spend every five dollars He puts in our pocket?

What do you do when you get a bonus at work or when an unexpected check arrives in the mail? If you are like most people, you celebrate! You go out to dinner and a movie or run out and buy that latest power tool or fancy fishing rod you've had your eye on. Maybe you make a down payment on the new car or new boat you've been drooling over. Meanwhile, unpaid bills pile up at home and you keep wondering how you are going to pay your debts. Why not use your bonus, or at least a large portion of it, to pay off some of those bills?

One of the bad things about debt is that the things we buy lose their luster so quickly. Spending money to pay for things we bought months ago is boring. We want to buy something new and fresh and exciting! So, we pull out the credit card and off we go again.

Another problem with getting out of debt is the allure of consolidation loans. Properly used, consolidation loans can be of benefit, particularly in lowering the amount of interest we pay, but there is a danger. Unless we exercise financial discipline, a consolidation loan will only make things worse. Eighty percent of people who get consolidation loans end up deeper in debt a year later. Why? Because the loan helped them free up some money, but they were not disciplined enough to keep from spending it. They said, "Oh! Extra money again! Let's go!"

Get God involved in your finances. He really is interested. Pray about your finances. Ask God for guidance and to reveal His will. Before you go shopping or before you make a purchase, especially a major purchase, take time to pray. Make sure you are doing the right thing before you proceed. "Come on, Hubbard, do you mean to tell me that God really cares whether I buy a new couch or not?" Yes, He cares because it involves His money. If you need a new couch, fine; I don't believe God has a problem with that. God doesn't care what kind of couch you buy, either, as long as it is not beyond your means. He doesn't care whether it's overstuffed, understuffed, pillow-fluffed, whether it has stripes or flowers, or whether it's brown or blue. What He does care about is whether or not this is the most responsible use of your money. Maybe it is. On the other hand, maybe you should consider keeping your old ratty couch for another year or two and pay off some debts instead.

One of the best ways to get God involved with our money is to get our money involved in God's investment program. As we have already seen, tithing is the first and most fundamental way to invest in the Kingdom of God. The Bible promises that if we give to God, we will receive back in good measure, pressed down, shaken together, and running over. Giving to God is a sure winner, a risk-free investment because we cannot outgive God. Whatever we give to Him, He will return to us in multiplied form. In America we can buy U.S. savings bonds, a guaranteed safe investment because they are backed up by the good faith and credit of the United States government. Giving to

God is even safer. His promise of a multiplied return is a biblical principle backed up by the good faith and credit of the Lord God Himself.

You might say, "That just doesn't make any sense to me. I have one thousand dollars and one thousand dollars' worth of bills to pay, and you want me to give one hundred dollars to the church? How can I afford to do that?" It's God's economy. We can't explain it; we just know it works. Get God involved in your finances. Take some of what He has given you and give it back as an investment in His Kingdom, and He will return it to you in multiplied form.

Over the years we've heard testimony after testimony of financial miracles, of how God completely turned around people's financial situations when they decided to get serious and get Him involved. It doesn't make sense to us either how we can take a dry, dead kernel of corn, bury it under some dirt and cow manure, and watch it spring up into a thousand kernels of corn. Somehow it works. Scientists can't even explain it. They can tell us *what* happens, but they can't tell us *how* it happens. It's a God thing. God said, "This is how it will be," and that's how it is. Don't try to explain it, analyze it, or dissect it; just do it. Do you want to get out of debt? Get God involved.

Get Wisdom

Secondly, after getting God involved, we need to *get wisdom*. King Solomon makes it clear that we need wisdom before we need money. The book of Proverbs states over and over that wisdom is of supreme value:

> *Blessed is the man who finds wisdom, the man who gains understanding, for she is more profitable than silver and yields better returns than gold. She is more precious than rubies; nothing you desire can compare with her.*
> Proverbs 3:13-14

> *Get wisdom, get understanding; do not forget my words or swerve from them. Do not forsake wisdom, and she will protect you; love her, and she will watch over you. Wisdom is supreme; therefore get wisdom. Though it cost all you have, get understanding.*
> Proverbs 4:5-7

Choose my instruction instead of silver, knowledge rather than choice gold, for wisdom is more precious than rubies, and nothing you desire can compare with her. Proverbs 8:10-11

How much better to get wisdom than gold, to choose understanding rather than silver! Proverbs 16:16

Wisdom is important, because without wisdom we will not properly manage our money. As we've said before, we both grew up poor. Ken started working when he was fourteen years old. Every day at two o'clock he got out of school, went to his job, and worked until ten. He even worked all day on Saturday. With his earnings, he helped pay the rent and bought his first car. By the time he was eighteen years old, he had an apartment of his own and two cars in the driveway. While he may have looked prosperous, he really didn't have a clue because he had never had anything. No one in either of our families growing up had anything. We never learned anything about money, because there was no need to; none of us had any. Then all of a sudden somebody started putting a paycheck in our hands. We were without wisdom, totally ignorant when it came to money. The only thing we knew to do with money was spend it.

No one ever taught us about savings accounts or investments or stocks or bonds. We had never heard of a 401(k) or an IRA. As far as we knew, a bank was just a place that got robbed. Nobody in our neighborhoods knew any of this either. We who were from the "wrong" side of the tracks never talked to the folks on the "right" side of the tracks who knew all of this stuff. We were ignorant for a long, long time. On getting our paychecks each week, we would then go out and do foolish things with the money because we lacked wisdom.

Proverbs 17:16 says, "Of what use is money in the hand of a fool, since he has no desire to get wisdom?" But where do you go to get wisdom? Ken tells about his early search for wisdom: "For a long time, I was too intimidated by the people who knew what I needed to know to talk to them. The times when I did ask, I often did not understand what they told me. I remember the first time I went into a bank and asked somebody about a CD. He started spouting off all this financial mumbojumbo that was like a foreign language to me. He could have been speaking Martian for all I knew. All I could do was sit there and try to act like I knew what was going on. When I walked out I was just as ignorant as when I walked in, except that now I was confused, too. I was still ignorant at twenty-one when I bought my first house. Interest rate? What's that? I just signed on the dotted line and was happy with my ten-point-nine-percent interest rate. By the time I bought my next house, I had learned how to get a better interest rate. At seven-point-three percent, I bought twice the house for the same monthly payment. As far as I was concerned, I had struck gold. I was still ignorant in many ways, but I was starting to learn."

There are a lot of people who are today where Ken was then. They have no money and have never had any money. When they get some money, they have no clue what to do with it, so they end up squandering it or frittering it away on a lot of nothing or getting themselves into debt for years to pay for something that will be gone in six months. Solomon said we need to get wisdom. It's not a matter of having a lot or a little. More money is never the solution to a financial problem. If you can't handle what you already have, what makes you think you could handle more? You say, "More money would sure help me out." To that we say, "How did you get where you are?" In some cases, the problem may be that you really don't have enough money. Most of the time, however, financial trouble is not a money problem, but a management problem.

Whatever else we do, we need to get wisdom. Proverbs 3:15 says that the value of wisdom is beyond compare, while Proverbs 4:7 asserts that wisdom is worth whatever price we have to pay. The turning point for you will come when you finally admit your financial ignorance and decide to take action. Instead of taking your paycheck and blowing it, invest forty or fifty dollars in some books on financial management. Read them and reread them; then go back and read them again. Gradually, you will begin to learn. You will see what you have been doing wrong and what you need to do to make it right.

Wisdom is worth buying, even though in reality, it is something we cannot buy. Wisdom comes through learning, through application of learning, and through experience. Even more, wisdom is a gift from God. James 1:5 says, "If any of you lacks wisdom, he should ask God, who gives generously to all without finding fault, and it will be given to him." I (Ken) continue to try to learn more and more. Even though I have come a long way from where I used to be, I am still a long way from where I want to be. Not long ago I paid to fly a man in to talk with me about financial matters, a man I regard as a financial genius. It cost me $247 for a round-trip airplane ticket. When he arrived, we sat down and I said, "Talk to me." For the next six hours he taught me a lot of terminology and what it meant, recommended books and other resources, and explained how to do many different things in the financial arena. That time was worth every penny I paid. Within weeks of that meeting I had already made up the cost in money I saved applying some of the things he taught me.

Do you want to get out of debt? Get wisdom. Do whatever you have to do, pay whatever you have to pay, change whatever you have to change in your life, but get wisdom. Don't keep going the same way you've always gone just because you think financial matters are beyond you. If we learned how to become better in our financial understanding and management, especially with our backgrounds, you can too.

Get Real

Thirdly, if you want to get out of debt, you've got to *get real*. Debt is serious business. If someone came in and offered to erase your debt right now, wouldn't you take that seriously? Don't take debt lightly. What we mean by "get real" is admit to yourself that you are not handling your money wisely. Acknowledge that your finances have gotten out of control and you need help. The first step to recovery is admitting the problem; seeking help is the second. We don't like to do that. So many of us are so insecure within ourselves that we don't want to say or do anything that will lead others to suspect that we don't have our act together. Don't pretend that you have everything under control when you don't. Identify your strengths and your weaknesses when it comes to money management, as well as those of your spouse. That way the two of you can work together, each of you playing on your respective strengths, to improve your financial management skills. Each marriage, each household, has to work out its own system based on the gifts, strengths, and weaknesses of each person involved.

In most households, one person tends to be more careful and frugal than the other. Sometimes it is due to personality, sometimes it is due to background, and it may be due to both. Even if you are very careful about money, you can still get into serious financial trouble if your spouse is a spender. The harder you work and the more you make, the more he or she spends. Let's face it, guys; it is not always the woman who spends all the money. It is common to stereotype the women as the ones who always grab the credit cards and run off on a shopping spree, but we men can be just as guilty.

If you are having financial problems, get real. Take a close, hard, honest look at your situation. If you have trouble controlling your spending, admit it. Take action. Seek help from someone you trust. Don't just sit there and do nothing. Proverbs 27:12 says, "The prudent see danger and take refuge, but the simple keep going and suffer for it." Sometimes we get this mentality: "I'm in debt and I always will be, so it doesn't really matter anyway." We think that if we ignore it, it will go away, but all that happens is we go deeper into debt. Get real. Get serious about getting out of debt.

Seven Steps in Debt Reduction

We want to share with you seven steps in debt reduction. This is by no means a complete list, just some practical ideas that might help. Some of them may fit your situation and some of them may not. Use them as they apply to you. Some of these tips may even spark ideas in your own mind of other things that will work. The important thing is to analyze your situation and take appropriate action.

1. Determine the source of the problem. Where are the problems with your finances? How did they arise? Don't be too quick to answer. Take time to figure out the source of the problem. Try to identify when, where, and how things first got off track. Are you undisciplined? Your spouse? Both of you? Was there a particular event or crisis that threw things off? Trace it back. "Oh, we made that bad decision two years ago." "It's all those school bills we're paying. What can we do to get rid of those?" "Remember that time you were out of work for six months?" Identify the problem. See if you can spot a trend of bad decisions or poor spending habits. Maybe you are simply working your way out of a one-time bad decision. On the other hand, the problem may be systemic. Whatever it is, nail it down and label it: "There's the problem!" Many times, identifying the source of the trouble is ninety percent of the battle.

2. Find support. If you are married, have a family discussion and discuss the changes and sacrifices that need to be made.

Agree that you will not use credit cards except in extreme emergency. You might consider the "frozen assets" strategy from chapter three of putting your credit cards in a bowl of water and freezing them. If credit card use is a real problem for you, some "plastic surgery" with your credit cards and a pair of scissors may be in order.

Husbands and wives should make themselves accountable to each other. We've heard that eighty-five percent of divorces occur over financial matters and often because one or the other or both are spending without the other's knowledge. When they come together in counseling, they each bring a mountain of debt that the other knew nothing about. It always amazes me when husbands and wives who are supposed to be "one" don't even know each other's financial business. If you are the spender in your family, admit it and get support from your spouse. There has been more than one man who's had to turn the credit cards over to his wife because he couldn't handle having them in his wallet.

Whether you are single or married, find support. Find someone who will be a prayer partner with you as you work to solve the problems, someone you trust outside your family that you can be accountable to. No one says you have to go through this alone, so don't even try. Set aside your pride and ask for help.

3. Create a spending plan. We recommend that you set up a spending plan rather than a budget. What's the difference? A budget tells you what you *can't* do while a spending plan tells you what you *can* do. It is always better to operate from the positive rather than the negative. Budgets tend to be very restrictive, making it easy to become depressed. A spending plan is much more optimistic, because it is based on what you have predetermined to be most important in your life. In other words, a spending plan helps you do all the things you want to do and that are most important to you because it is designed to give those things priority.

Of course, ongoing monthly bills and other necessary expenses obviously are included, but don't neglect those areas of personal enrichment, those hobbies or activities that add spice and fulfillment to life. That list could include just about anything:

golfing, fishing, hunting, Scouting, coaching Little League, book clubs, charities, magazines, coin collecting, stamp collecting, etc. The challenge comes in identifying the most important items and focusing on them, since few of us will ever have the time or money to do everything we would like to do. Build your spending plan around those predetermined choices. For example, if you decide that golfing is your main outside interest, then your extra money will go to golfing; it won't go to softball, fishing, hunting, whitewater rafting, or parasailing. Create a spending plan and predetermine where your money is going to go.

Another important part of creating a successful spending plan is knowing the difference between needs, wants, and desires. Needs are those things that are essential for life: food, water, clothing, shelter, etc. Wants are choices we make regarding the quality of our needs. We need food, but a want would be whether to eat a hot dog or a steak. Desires are everything else: I desire to have a new car or a new boat. I desire to pursue this hobby. The priority order of the three should be self-evident. In any sensible spending plan, needs come first, followed by wants (how fancy do we want to be in supplying our needs?), and finally, desires.

4. List your debts. Define the problem. List each of your debts, whether loans, credit cards, car or house payments, or whatever, along with the full balances, minimum monthly payments, and interest rates of each. Just get it in front of you. It's amazing how much confusion disappears just by knowing where you stand. Categorize your bills. Determine which ones need to be paid now and which ones can wait. If possible, target the bills with the highest interest rates first, because they are the ones costing you the most money. Develop a payment plan of some kind and keep it as simple as possible. Make it adequate for your situation but no more complicated than necessary. Almost any plan is better than no plan at all. Update your list and evaluate your progress regularly. Keeping a clear picture of your financial situation before you will help you maintain control and make solid progress toward getting out of debt.

5. Be ready for a lifestyle change. If you always do what you've always done, you'll always get what you've always had. If your finances are not working, something has to change. Change is hard, especially when we have grown truly fond of things the way they are and don't want to give anything up. It boils down to this: Which do you want more, to hold onto your current lifestyle even though it's dragging you down financially, or to get out of debt? The choice is yours. You've got to give up to go up. It's either play now and pay later (possibly for the rest of your life) or pay now and play later. If your outgo exceeds your income, you have to cut spending. There is no other way to balance things out. As a general rule, try to create a spending plan that has no more than seventy percent of your take-home income going into daily living expenses. In other words, set your goal to live on seventy percent of what you make (this includes your tithe). The remaining thirty percent is a cushion.

Get sensible about handling your debt payments. Even an extra $25.00 a month applied to debt can make a big difference. Here is an example. A $5,000 debt at twenty-one percent interest will take twenty years to pay off at the minimum payment amount. Paying just $25.00 a month more to that debt—$25.00 above the minimum payment—will retire that entire debt in less than nine years rather than twenty and cost $8,800 instead of $13,000. In another example, making just one extra mortgage payment a year will knock seven years off your mortgage. All of this is nothing other than good common sense. It is wisdom.

6. Consolidate several debts. Be careful with this one. In some cases a consolidation loan can be very useful, particularly in helping you get a better focus. If you have a lot of little debts that are eating you up with interest every month and are hard to keep track of, consolidating them into one loan with one monthly payment may be easier to manage. You may also get a better overall interest rate.

Having said that, I have to emphasize that you can never borrow your way out of debt. Consolidation is not a magic formula. It is not a genie that will come out of a bottle and say, "Poof! Your debt is all gone." It is a tool, nothing more. Used prudently, it can simplify the task of getting out of debt. Just remember that a consolidation loan is itself a debt that must be paid.

7. Use special money to pay off debt. By special money we mean bonuses, birthday money, overtime pay, garage sale proceeds, income from odd jobs or secondary employment. When I (Ken) first started in ministry, I really struggled to get by on my paycheck every week. To me, it wasn't enough money. On my day off I went knocking on doors looking for odd jobs to supplement my income. Here I was, a "dignified" pastor seeking menial work to put a few more dollars in my pocket. I went to a senior citizens' retirement village and asked residents if I could clean out their gutters. I got $30.00 per house for about thirty minutes of work at each place. I made some good money and applied it toward a silly debt that I had gotten into.

In my family, there are two specific areas where we have decided to focus our extra money: our house and our vacations. We like putting money into our home because we know that we will get some of it back, like landscaping, decorating, remodeling, whatever. We also take our vacations as a family. It has become our tradition to make each vacation a learning experience with a specific theme. For example, one of our recent vacations focused on the Revolutionary War.

All the money that I get from guest speaking, camps, conventions, etc., I consider as income from my "side job." That is the money I use to invest in those things that I like. All I'm saying is that when you get extra money, don't use it to get deeper in debt. Use it to pay a bill or set it aside for one of the things that you really want to do. Be sensible. Don't throw that extra money away like corn scattered on the gravel.

Getting out of debt is never easy, but neither is it impossible. It requires discipline, commitment, clear-headed thinking, and a plan of action. Get God involved, get wisdom, and get real. Make the determination that, next to your tithe, getting out of debt is your top financial priority. Create a workable, reasonable spending plan. Get your debts clearly before you and plan your attack. Pray for wisdom and for the Lord to lead you and show you what to do and where to turn. Lastly, don't wait another day to get started. There is no better time to begin getting out of debt than right now. Don't delay. Start today.

CHAPTER TEN

PREPARING FOR FAMINE

What would you do if disaster struck? How well would you handle things if the bottom suddenly fell out of your life? Are you prepared financially for emergencies and the unexpected? What if you suddenly lost your job? What if you or your spouse was diagnosed with cancer? What if someone in your family was seriously injured in an accident, with recovery a long, slow, and costly process? If you suddenly and unexpectedly found yourself totally dependent on your own financial reserves and resources, how long would they last? Why worry? After all, such tragedies always happen to "the other guy," don't they?

Do they? These scenarios are not as far-fetched or unlikely as we like to think. If worse came to worst, how long could you survive financially on what you have in savings? If you are like most Americans, not very long. Ninety percent of Americans have a thousand dollars or less in savings. That's pretty scary, particularly considering that we live in one of the most affluent nations in the world. We may be affluent, but we are also a nation of spenders. Our free-spending ways start at the top and affect every class and level of society. In America, our national debt *alone* exceeds the gross national product of many of the world's other nations. We Americans tend to be free-wheeling, free-spending, live-for-the-moment type of people who give little thought to the future, at least where money is concerned. More and more, ours is an "eat drink and be merry for tomorrow we die" philosophy, and our spending habits prove it.

Part of the reason for this lack of concern for the future stems from the fact that two generations of people have now grown up under the ominous shadow of the nuclear mushroom cloud. Why plan seriously for the future if the world could blow up tomorrow? An increasing number of people in our society find no significant meaning or purpose in life. Why not take whatever they can get of its pleasures while they have the chance? After all, life is short. Get all the gusto you can.

Another factor in our national obsession with the present is living under an economy that is driven by consumer credit. Easy and widely available credit has made us an impatient people. No longer do we have to wait while saving for weeks, months, or even years in order to buy something we want. Today, armed with a walletfull of credit cards, we can "buy" virtually whatever we want, whenever we want, whether or not we can afford it, and have it right now. It's the "play now, pay later" philosophy, with the emphasis squarely on "play now." We're so busy playing and partying and trying to keep up with the Joneses that we forget that payday is coming. When payday does come—and it always comes—it usually hits hard. Whether it is the sudden realization of out-of-control debt or an unexpected calamity, payday catches many of us completely unprepared.

What will you do when famine comes? By "famine," we mean any unanticipated disaster, tragedy, hardship, or reversal of fortune that suddenly dries up your personal resources. A famine could be just about anything: a death in the family, a devastating fire, job loss, a major health crisis, anything that puts a sudden drain on your financial resources. What if the crisis comes and you have no assets with which to meet it? Have you ever tried to draw water from an empty well?

Rest assured, famine *will* come. It's inevitable. Eventually, all of us who live long enough will face the famine of old age. What will you do when you can no longer physically do what you are getting paid to do now? Are you financially set for retirement? Perhaps you are a gifted musician. What happens if arthritis attacks your fingers so you can no longer play the guitar or the keyboard? Famine comes. Maybe you are a speaker or maybe you can sing like an angel. What happens if you lose your voice? Famine comes.

Famine may come also in the form of tragedy or disaster. Let's say that you are the primary breadwinner in your family. What happens if you lose your job or, worse, become permanently disabled? Famine comes. Earthquake, fire, flood, divorce, death of a spouse—any of these could reverse your financial situation literally overnight. Famine comes. Your furnace goes out. Your water heater goes out. Your car breaks down. Any of these could be famine if you are not prepared to deal with them.

Being prepared is the key. No matter how hard we try or how much we might wish it were otherwise, we cannot avoid famine. Sometime or another, famine of some kind will come into our lives. Wisdom would say that since we can't avoid famine, we should do everything we can to prepare for it.

Why Prepare for Famine?

The unfortunate truth is that many churches and many, many people are not financially prepared for famine. On the average, middle-class Christians in America today, if forced to live off their stored resources, could go no longer than two or three months without getting into severe financial hardship. Why? Either we have bought into the popular culture and its "play now, pay later" philosophy and spend our money as soon as we get it, or we have been persuaded by the erroneous teaching that says Christians shouldn't have much money because it will tempt us away from God. Another possibility is ignorance. Some of you may be like the two of us and grew up never being taught anything about financial management. You can't hold on to money because you don't know how.

Spiritual ignorance may also be a factor. Ignorance of the things of God will separate us from the blessings of God. God wants to bless us financially, but if we do not understand His principles of tithing, investing, and avoiding debt, we essentially tie His hands and He can do little for us. Meanwhile, the secular world makes all the money while we sit back wringing our hands and wondering where the rent money is coming from, or the money to repair the church air conditioner.

This is not the way it should be. As the Body of Christ, the Church should have everything it needs to fulfill His commission. Think of it this way. When God created our physical bodies, He gave them the ability biologically to reproduce, to be self-repairing, and to be self-sufficient. Everything we need to survive, thrive, grow, and be fruitful and productive was put in us at the very beginning. Prior to the fall, the human body was designed to last forever. By design, Adam was all-sufficient, just like his Creator.

The Body of Christ is the same way, or should be. As Christians, born-again followers of Christ, we are part of a great spiritual family, which the apostle Paul aptly describes as a body. A well-functioning body has everything it needs: All the body parts are present and performing their respective functions. Likewise, the Body of Christ, in order to be healthy, needs every member present and functioning. A healthy church, like a health body, should reproduce, regularly bringing new people into the fellowship of faith in Christ. A healthy church should be self-repairing: If something breaks, it should be fixed. If fellowship and harmony break down, the church should have the internal resources to repair the breach. If a member of the body is broken or injured, the rest of the body should be able to bring healing. A healthy church should be self-sufficient, containing within itself everything it needs to function and carry out its Christ-ordained mission.

What this means in practical terms is that any need in the church should be able to be met by those who are in the church. Does it ever bother you that churches so often have to go to secular institutions to get construction loans, building-improvement loans, and the like? It bothers us. Judging from the New Testament example, we believe that Christ's ideal for His Church is that any need in the body, whether personal or corporate, should be met with resources that are within the body. Ideally, it should never be necessary for the church to go to outside sources, particularly secular ones, for assistance. The Bible says that we are to be the lenders, not the borrowers. If we would learn to do things according to God's plan, we believe that they would come to us for money. This is one reason why we should prepare for famine, so that when it comes, we will be in a position to lend—to assist and give help—rather than to borrow or depend on others for help.

We should not have to go to the secular institutions to get what the body needs. The body of Christ ought to be self-sufficient, meeting its own needs from within. The reason we are not so often is because we do not practice God's principles. Preparing for famine is important because we need to be ready for whatever the Lord may ask of us. He may want us to be like the Good Samaritan, paying for the needs of another out of our own resources. Could you do that right now if the occasion arose?

There are those who would argue against the need for us to prepare for famine. "After all," they would say, "didn't Jesus tell us in Matthew chapter 6 not to worry about what we wear, what we eat, and all of those things?" Our response is, "Yes, He did. Absolutely." Jesus was saying that we should trust God to meet our everyday needs and that there is no reason for us to worry. Worry reflects lack of faith.

Why then should we plan for famine? First of all, if we have a plan, we will be less inclined to worry. If we have made preparations ahead of time and know what to do when trouble comes, we will be more confident and at peace when dealing with life. Second, planning for famine is a good idea as long as we understand that we cannot count on those plans alone to bring us through. That's what Jesus means in Matthew 6. Money alone will not help us. God will see us through, but wise preparation is always in order. We plan for famine, but we trust in the Lord.

Forgetting the Abundance

The story of Joseph in the book of Genesis is a wonderful story in many ways. Among other things, it is a perfect illustration of the value and importance of preparing for famine. As prime minister of Egypt and second to Pharaoh, Joseph's wise planning and administration during seven years of plenty kept the Egyptian people from starving during the seven years of famine that followed. We want to suggest that for our purposes here, Joseph symbolizes the Church and the way we ought to be in the world.

We're sure you remember the story. Young Joseph, sold into slavery by his jealous brothers, ended up as a slave in the house of Potiphar, captain of the guard for Pharaoh. He quickly acquired a reputation as an excellent administrator of Potiphar's estate. Falsely accused of sexual assault by Potiphar's wife because he refused her advances, Joseph spent several years in prison, where again he became known for his administrative ability as the warden's assistant. While in prison, Joseph also gained a reputation as an interpreter of dreams. The day came when Pharaoh himself had a troubling dream—two dreams, in fact—and needed someone to explain them to him. Upon hearing of Joseph and his interpretive skills, Pharaoh summoned him.

When Joseph came before Pharaoh, the Egyptian king related his dreams. In one dream, seven healthy cows walked out of the Nile, followed by seven lean and scrawny cows. The seven scrawny cows ate the seven healthy cows, but remained as scrawny as ever. The second dream was similar, except that this time seven healthy heads of grain were consumed by seven thin, weary heads of grain.

Joseph listened carefully, and then spoke as God gave him the interpretation:

> *Then Joseph said to Pharaoh, "The dreams of Pharaoh are one and the same. God has revealed to Pharaoh what he is about to do. The seven good cows are seven years, and the seven good heads of grain are seven years; it is one and the same dream. The seven lean, ugly cows that came up afterward are seven years, and so are the seven worthless heads of grain scorched by the east wind: They are seven years of famine. It is just as I said to Pharaoh: God has shown Pharaoh what he is about to do. Seven years of great abundance are coming throughout the land of Egypt, but seven years of famine will follow them. Then all the abundance in Egypt will be forgotten, and the famine will ravage the land. The abundance in the land will not be remembered, because the famine that follows it will be so severe. The reason the dream was given to Pharaoh in two forms is that the matter has been firmly decided by God, and God will do it soon. And now let Pharaoh look for a discerning and wise man and put him in charge of the land of Egypt."*
>
> Genesis 41:25-33

For seven years Egypt would enjoy great abundance. Every harvest would be a bumper crop. The nation would know prosperity as never before. Life for the Egyptians would be better than they had ever experienced before. After seven years, however, those golden days would end and the nation would be seized by a famine more severe than any other in living memory. The famine would be so bad that the people, in their suffering, would forget all about the abundance of the seven good years.

There is a lesson here for us. All the abundance will be forgotten. This is a critical point. In America today we are spending money like

144

crazy. We get a $5,000 raise and instead of investing it or saving it, we buy a new car. We think, "With my raise, now I can go up to the next level." That's dangerous thinking. Debt has nothing to do with how much we make, but with how much we spend. If God is God enough to take care of us at $20,000, He's God enough to take care of us at $100,000. He might give us a $10,000 raise to see what we will do with it. If we prove to be profitable servants, He will make sure we get more. But the problem is that we keep spending at the level of our income. It is impossible for us ever to become profitable spending that way. By spending everything we make, we are forgetting the abundance and, even worse, laying aside nothing to carry us through lean times.

If we eat everything we have and don't save any kernels of corn to put back in the ground, we are forgetting the abundance. It doesn't matter how much we gorge ourselves now; somewhere down the line, if we haven't put something back in the ground, we are going to get hungry again. During the lean times, we will forget what the T-bone steaks and barbecued ribs tasted like because the only thing we will have is hot dogs. When you're hungry, just about anything looks good. Odds are that when the prodigal son was sitting in that pigsty with his stomach growling after his third day without food, those dry husks the pigs were eating began to look like a feast to him. He forgot the abundance of his wild days spending his wealth. It was only after he came to his senses that he was able to remember how good things were at home.

In America today we are spending money faster than we get it. Some of us don't have a clue what we're doing. We don't even care how much money we spend. All we do is get ourselves further in debt to satisfy our cravings. We are forgetting the abundance. We are living in a time right now when we are squandering away our wealth. When the day of famine comes, we won't even remember all the great things we had. All we will know is that right now we are broke, busted, and disgusted. With no money, it won't matter at all how well we ate back then. The severity of our needs will cause us to forget the blessings. That's when we start blaming God. "How come God doesn't ever come through for me? Why doesn't God ever bless me?" He did. The problem is that we forgot the blessings in the face of the famine. Don't forget the abundance.

Put Something Aside for a Bad Year

After interpreting Pharaoh's dream, Joseph gave him a sound piece of advice: "And now let Pharaoh look for a discerning and wise man and put him in charge of the land of Egypt" (Genesis 41:33). God will always invest in a discerning and wise man. God plays the stock market. He will invest a little in you; if you prove faithful, He will invest more. Seven years of abundance would be followed by seven years of famine. God will always invest something in you. He will never create a famine without first investing in you everything you need to withstand it. He won't; that's not His character. If a flood is coming, He will invest in you and help you build an ark before it arrives. Before famine comes, God will invest in you and what you do with that investment is vitally important to your success. God's investment in you is important, but what you do with it is even more important. Don't forget about His investment in you. Don't forget the abundance.

Not only did God give Joseph the interpretation of Pharaoh's dreams; He also gave him an economic plan that will still work today:

> "And now let Pharaoh look for a discerning and wise man and put him in charge of the land of Egypt. Let Pharaoh appoint commissioners over the land to take a fifth of the harvest of Egypt during the seven years of abundance. They should collect all the food of these good years that are coming and store up the grain under the authority of Pharaoh, to be kept in the cities for food. This food should be held in reserve for the country, to be used during the seven years of famine that will come upon Egypt, so that the country may not be ruined by the famine." The plan seemed good to Pharaoh and to all his officials. So Pharaoh asked them, "Can we find anyone like this man, one in whom is the spirit of God?" Then Pharaoh said to Joseph, "Since God has made all this known to you, there is no one so discerning and wise as you. You shall be in charge of my palace, and all my people are to submit to your orders. Only with respect to the throne will I be greater than you." So Pharaoh said to Joseph, "I hereby put you in charge of the whole land of Egypt."
>
> Genesis 41:33-41

Joseph's counsel to Pharaoh was to hold in reserve one fifth of each harvest during the seven years of abundance to provide food during the years of famine. This illustrates a sound principle for planning for famine: *Never let a good year pass without putting something aside for a bad year.* Breaking it down a little further, never let a paycheck pass through your hands without taking something out of it to hold against the famine that will surely come.

Don't let yourself get caught in the "someday syndrome": "Someday things will be better. Someday I'm going to have money. Someday I'm going to get out of debt." Let "someday" start today. Develop the habit now with every paycheck of paying God first (the tithe); then give Uncle Sam his cut (withholdings and Social Security). The third person you should pay is *yourself.* Set aside a specific percentage of your income as a reserve against famine. Joseph suggested that Pharaoh hold back one fifth of the harvest for that purpose. That may be a good rule of thumb for us as well.

If you are in the financial position to do so, you may want to consider setting aside twenty percent (onefifth) of your income. That means, don't spend it. Deposit it into a special savings account, money market account, CD, or other similar instrument where it can earn interest. Perhaps you can't afford to set aside twenty percent right now. That's okay. Take a close look at your situation and decide what you *can* afford. Can you reserve fifteen percent, ten percent, five percent? Any amount is better than no amount. The important thing is to begin right away. Take action now. There is no better time than the present.

Don't think that you have to make more money before you can sock some away. If you think that way, you will never do anything. It doesn't matter how much you make; put some of it away. Don't wait until you get to the next level. Don't wait for your next raise or your next bonus. Don't wait for your next job or your next house before you start to set aside some of your income. Take advantage of the good years while you have them. Otherwise, you will be sixty years old and still waiting to get to the place where you can begin planning for famine. Remember that you can be profitable at any level. It is your attitude that counts, not the amount of your bank account.

Don't think that you are too old or have waited too long. It's never too late to start. Anything you can do now will go a long way for you in the future. The only thing that can hurt you is to do nothing. If you can't set aside twenty percent right now, then set aside what you can and make twenty percent your goal.

Another "famine plan," which is also just a good all-around financial plan, is the 10-10-80 plan. This simply means, pay God ten percent, pay yourself ten percent (your set-aside) and live on 80%. Perhaps that breakdown isn't possible for you right now. You may have to pay off some debts first to free up some assets. Make 10-10-80 your goal to work toward.

We can guarantee you that if you will commit yourself to one of these plans (or another of your choosing, as long as it follows the same general principles), God will honor your faithfulness and start to turn things around in your life. He will know that you are a profitable servant who will bring a good return, and He will invest more heavily in you. You will be amazed at the spiritual miracles that will happen in your life not only in the area of finances, but in other areas as well.

This is not wishful thinking but a solid biblical principle. Take it from us; we have seen it in action in our own lives as well as in the lives of others. When I (Ken) was growing up, we thought we were doing well if we had enough money to pay the rent. I still remember my mother coming home from work at night exhausted, absolutely whipped, taking her $2.25-an-hour wages and her tip money and placing them in a jar she kept hidden in the bottom drawer of her dresser so we could pay the rent.

The point we are making is that we did not come by financial knowledge naturally. We were not born with silver spoons in our mouths. Everything we know we had to learn on our own after we were grown. These are God's principles—God's system—and they are found in His Word. We didn't start learning God's Word so that I could impress people with my knowledge. We started learning God's word because we couldn't afford to pay a financial adviser.

These principles work. Never let a good year pass without putting something aside for a bad year. Don't let a paycheck go by without putting something aside for the day when famine comes.

Be Ready When the Time Comes

None of us knows when famine will strike in our lives. The best we can do is pray, stay alert, and apply God's principles to help us prepare. It's impossible to foresee or plan for every contingency, but having some of our resources laid up in reserve against the unexpected will give us flexibility when we need it. In the same way, we cannot know when God will bring across our path someone who needs our help. Have you ever thought that *you* might be God's answer for someone else's famine? Famine struck that man on the Jericho-Jerusalem road who was attacked by thieves, stripped, robbed, beaten, and left half dead. For him, relief came from an unexpected source: a Samaritan who had not only the compassion to help, but also the financial and material means to do so. Whose Good Samaritan will you be? You will never know until the time comes. If you have a reserve laid up, you will be in a position to bless the person God brings across your path.

Such readiness will never happen without deliberate, conscious planning. Christians caught in the "someday syndrome" will never be ready. For them, financial stability is always off in some indefinite future that they are wistfully waiting for "someday." Do you think Joseph whiled away his hours in Potiphar's house or in prison simply dreaming of the "someday" when things would be better? We don't think so. For many years, Joseph's situation seemed pretty grim, but he never let it stop him. He determined to do what he could where he was with what he had. Joseph did not wait until he got to "the next level" before he planted his seeds and invested his assets, meager as they might have seemed at the time. Because Joseph was faithful, determined to turn a profit wherever he was, God kept His hand on him and prospered him wherever he was—even in prison. From the beginning, Joseph laid up for himself reserves of faithfulness, obedience, and integrity that bore fruit at the proper time. When the opportunity came, Joseph was ready.

Pharaoh was astute enough to recognize that the same man who suggested the strategy to prepare for famine was also the man best suited to implement it. He immediately promoted Joseph to be his right-hand man, his second in command, and placed him in charge of the entire country. Talk about a rags-to-riches story! In the space of no more than a couple of hours Joseph was raised from the status of imprisoned slave to prime minister of Egypt! Of course, Joseph's "overnight success" required twenty years of patient, faithful, and obedient service. During that time he did not fritter away his time, his talents, or his resources, but worked hard to lay up "treasures in Heaven" against the day when God would raise him up. When that day came, Joseph was ready. God not only blessed Joseph, but put Joseph in a position where he could bless many others from the store he had laid up for twenty years. Because Joseph was faithful during his own years of famine, God raised him up to be instrumental in saving millions of Egyptians from starvation during a literal famine.

God gave Joseph an economic plan that brought Egypt through a severe crisis. As a result of Joseph's capable administration and the investment of his time, energy, and talent over many years, Egypt grew in prosperity. Four hundred years later when the Israelite slaves (who were descendants of Joseph and his brothers) left Egypt under Moses, they departed heavy-laden with the gold of Egypt, which was an abundant return on the investment Joseph had made centuries before. Because of Joseph's faithfulness, two entire nations were blessed: Egypt during his own day, and Israel four centuries later. By extension, Joseph's faithfulness in preparing for famine has blessed the entire world, because through Israel came Jesus Christ, the Son of God and Savior of the world. Don't ever think for a moment that your investment doesn't matter! Only God knows what it can do!

We said earlier that for our purposes, Joseph represents what the Church ought to be. We believe that the Church ought to be so blessed, so abundant in prosperity (spiritual as well as financial), that the secular world would look to us for the standard rather than the other way around. The hand of God ought to be so clearly on us that they will seek us out and ask, "What is the secret of your success?" We believe that when the children of the King start living like children of the King instead of like paupers in the gutter, the world will sit up and take notice. They will know that something is different about us. They may not all like it, but they won't be able to ignore it. Think of the difference it could make in our world if the Church as a whole really did become the leader rather than the follower and the lender rather than the borrower!

Joseph was able to get Egypt's economy strong enough that it could withstand a famine. That is my challenge to you as well. Learn and apply God's financial principles in your own life and situation so that when famine comes, you will be able not only to endure, but also to prosper in the midst of it. Start laying aside now for the future so that when the time comes that God wants to elevate you, you will be ready.

You should become such a rock of stability that when the storms hit, friends and neighbors will automatically turn to you for counsel and encouragement because they see the strength in your life and know that God is its source.

Remember the "Golden Rule"

The first principle of planning for famine is to *never let a good year pass without putting something back for a bad year.* That relates directly to a second principle: *put your money to work,* which we have already looked at in the chapters on tithing and investing. A third important principle to keep in mind when planning for famine is the "golden rule." We're not talking about the biblical golden rule, "Do unto others as you would have them do unto you," although that is certainly always applicable, even in the world of finances. No, we're talking about the "golden rule" of finance: *He who has the gold makes the rules.*

We realize that does not sound very spiritual, but it is true. Money talks. People with money get the ear of political and civic leaders. We guarantee you that a church with two million dollars in the bank that it is looking to invest will have influence in its community. If you walk into a car dealership or a real estate office with cash in hand, you will have more clout than someone else who will need bank financing. When you already have money, you can make better deals.

Having a reserve of cash on hand will enable you to take advantage of quick opportunities. A bank forecloses on a house and you can step right in and buy it. Someone needs to sell his car quickly because he is moving, and you can take it off his hands right away.

If that sounds unfriendly, just remember that the Bible says that the wealth of the wicked is laid up for the righteous. Why should the secular, ungodly institutions and power structures of the world continue to have all the money? Think of the difference it would make if committed Christian people controlled more of the world's wealth— people committed not to the satisfaction of their own greed, lusts, and desires, but committed to the purposes of God and the cause of His Kingdom in the world.

That is why we need to be committed as believers to planning for famine: not only to get ourselves through the tough times that will come, but also to be a source of blessing and stability for others and to advance the cause of Christ in the world. Let's get our heads out of the sand and the devil out of our checkbooks. It's never too late to turn around and start over. Start applying God's financial principles to your life and watch what happens. You won't believe the difference it will make. God wants to bless you. He wants you to prosper. He wants you to make a difference in your world and bless the people around you. Begin today laying aside part of your means against future famine. Invest yourself faithfully where you are with what you have right now so that when the time comes for God to elevate you, you will be ready.

CHAPTER ELEVEN

SLAVING, SAVING, AND SHIFTING

A Christian who continually experiences financial difficulty is a Christian whose life is out of balance. Our churches are filled with believers who whoop and holler and sing and dance and worship and praise the Lord like nobody's business, but who go home to an unending grind of simply trying to make ends meet, of always having too much month left at the end of the money. They are afraid to answer the phone for fear it will be another bill collector. At church and at home they pray for help and claim that God will supply all their needs, yet nothing ever changes.

We need balance in our lives as believers. If we want something to come down from Heaven, we have to send something up. It's a two-way ladder. Are you struggling in some area of your life? Quit waiting on God to bless you; start blessing God. Stop waiting for God to say good things about you; start saying good things about God. "I need somebody to love me." Then love God. "I need somebody to bless me." Then bless God. "I have a financial problem." Then give to God. We spend so much time asking, asking, asking that we forget to send something up. We're looking for a harvest when we've never planted any seeds. Whatever we plant in Heaven will yield an abundant harvest— sometimes on earth—and "a good measure, pressed down, shaken together and running over, will be poured into [our] lap" (Luke 6:38).

That verse has to do with a lot more than just money. It relates to every area of our life: our worship life, our service life, our family life, our professional life, our financial life, and our private life. Generosity is a lifestyle. When we give from our heart—whatever the gift—we give to Heaven and God will honor our gift. Every gift we give out of love and compassion is a seed planted in Heaven that will eventually yield a harvest. We cannot outgive God, but if we hope to receive, we have to offer up. That's part of where balance comes in.

We need balance between praise and principle. If things are not in balance, then God cannot build on them. It's perfectly fine to sing and dance and shout to the Lord, but we need to exercise some solid, practical principles also. We can't simply worship our way through every problem in life. We must apply the biblical principles that God has given us. At the same time, we can't live on just a steady diet of principles with no praise. Principles give us grounding and stability, while praise gives us perspective and energy. Principles feed us, while praise fills our cup. A healthy Christian life and a healthy church need balance between the two.

Another area where we need balance is in our relationships. Of course, the most fundamental and important relationship we have is our relationship with God. When we repented of our sins and placed our faith in Jesus Christ as our Savior and Lord, He brought us into a right relationship with His Father. As important as that relationship is, our lives will still be out of balance if we focus all our attention on our relationship with God and neglect the other relationships of our lives. It's great to praise and worship God, but we still have to pay our bills. Husbands still have to love their wives and wives still have to honor their husbands. Parents still have to respect their children and children still have to respect their parents.

Carpenters use a level to make sure that boards and beams are in balance. A building that is not level is in trouble. Likewise, our lives are in trouble if we are not in balance or "on the level." People are watching us. If they see us worshiping and having a great time in the Lord and talking about all God has done for us, while all the while we owe them fifty dollars from two years ago, what kind of message do we send them? We are off-balance, out of level, and have no foundation for talking with them about the things of God. If we try to, they're liable to say, "What kind of Christian are you? You don't even pay your bills on time."

When we get saved, every relationship in our lives should change.

Our relationship with God should change. Our relationship with our spouse should change. Our relationship with our children should change. Our relationship with our parents should change. Our relationship with our boss should change. Don't think of your job as just something you do to get a paycheck. Think of it as work done as unto the Lord. Instead of complaining about your boss or about how bad conditions are or how underpaid you are, set yourself a goal to be the best worker in that place because you are working not for a company but for God. If you simply can't take it any more, at least show the integrity to give a two-week notice before you leave. Being saved changes our relationships.

Our relationship to money also has to change. If your philosophy about money is the same now as it was before you were saved, then something is wrong. The first thing that ought to change in your attitude toward money is your attitude toward the tithe. Very simply, tithing is the right thing to do, so do it. The second thing that ought to change is your understanding that God expects you to turn a profit. That goes back to the whole idea of giving and investing, making the most of your opportunities to multiply what God has given you.

Being saved changes our relationships. Something is wrong if we are still doing everything in the same vein as we did before we were saved. We need to take care that our relationships are in balance. Our future blessings and our future success are directly affected by the balance we maintain in our relationships both with God and with others.

No More Empty Hands

When our lives are in balance, God can bless us the way He wants to. He can invest in our lives knowing that we will be faithful to turn a profit and bring a good return. Because He owns all things, He can turn hearts and events to bring the wealth of the world into the hands of His faithful people. This is exactly what He did for the Israelites just before they left Egypt. When God delivered them from slavery, He did not lead them out of Egypt empty-handed:

> *"And I will make the Egyptians favorably disposed toward this*
> *people, so that when you leave you will not go empty-handed.*
> *Every woman is to ask her neighbor and any woman living in*

her house for articles of silver and gold and for clothing, which you will put on your sons and daughters. And so you will plunder the Egyptians."   Exodus 3:21-22

The Israelites did as Moses instructed and asked the Egyptians for articles of silver and gold and for clothing. The LORD had made the Egyptians favorably disposed toward the people, and they gave them what they asked for; so they plundered the Egyptians.   Exodus 12:35-36

That very night the Israelites—probably three million strong—walked out of Egypt not as slaves but as free people. In their arms they carried the wealth of Egypt—the same wealth that Joseph had helped make possible by his wise administration four hundred years earlier. Not long after, some of that wealth was used to make the golden calf that many of the Israelites worshiped while Moses was on Mount Sinai receiving the Law from the Lord. This just goes to show that wealth can be used for evil purposes. Later on, however, the people freely and generously gave much of this wealth from Egypt for use in building the Tabernacle and its furnishings, which some experts have estimated would be worth 87 billion dollars in today's currency.

If we view the Israelites as an Old Testament picture of the Church, we can get an idea of what God desires for us today. He does not want us to go through life with perpetually empty arms. He wants to bless us. His desire is that we prosper and turn a profit, and we can do neither if we are broke. Isn't it amazing how as New Testament believers we can shout and dance about freedom in Christ, yet still be enslaved to debt and mired in financial bondage? Many of us have been taught to accept poverty or financial leanness as the norm and that we should be satisfied with our spiritual freedom in Christ and patiently wait for our "pie in the sky by and by."

Certainly, being set free from our sins by the blood of Christ is of first importance. At the same time, I believe that when God liberates us, He wants to liberate us completely. Why would He wish to set our spirits free from bondage to sin and Satan, yet leave our finances in bondage to those same forces? It just doesn't make sense. If we are in financial bondage, it is not because God wants us there but because we put ourselves there by our own choices.

Wealth itself is immaterial to God. Since He owns everything anyway, He has no need of money. It is no big deal to Him. Our attitude toward money, on the other hand, is a big deal to Him because it reveals where our heart is. Money is a commodity, the medium of exchange that we use to get things done in the world. It can be used for God's glory just as easily as it can be used to serve the devil. If we prove ourselves faithful to God and free of any allegiance to money, God has no problem with letting us have it—sometimes a lot of it—because He knows we will handle it wisely.

We believe the day is coming when the Church of Jesus Christ will experience a general "financial revival." More and more churches and individual believers will step out of famine into a new day of prosperity. Here is why I believe this. Jesus is coming back, and I believe He is coming soon. I also believe that when He comes back, it will not be to rescue a struggling, poverty-stricken Church that is hurting and barely hanging on against a ravening world. On the contrary, I believe He is going to "rescue" the world from the Church. I believe the Church will have the devil "on the ropes." Christ is going to "rescue" the devil from a radical generation of Christians. When we leave, we will not leave empty-handed.

Before Christ returns, we're going to need some of that "green stuff," money, gold, wealth, whatever you want to call it. I believe that as we approach these last days and the great last-days revival comes, we Christians are going to have to learn to store up treasures for ourselves in Heaven. We are going to have to learn to be good stewards and financial managers to handle treasures that we are going to need right now: more buildings and buses and Bible schools to reach and train the great influx of new believers that will come in as a result of the revival. God is laying up the wealth of the wicked for the righteous. A great divine financial transfer is going to take place, and there will be a great need for Christians who know how to handle money, be wise investors, and exercise good stewardship. We Christians must learn how to dream again and then put into practice the biblical principles that will help us finance those dreams.

One of the first things we have to learn in this process is how to shift from *slaving* to *saving*.

Slaving

To better understand what we mean by "slaving," let's return to the story of the Israelites in Egypt. Here were the children of Israel, the people of God, toiling in Pharaoh's mud pits to make bricks for his incessant building projects. They were up before dawn every day, slaving away beneath the scorching sun under the whips and the curses of their Egyptian taskmasters. At sunset, they would drag home and fall into their beds, only to be up again the next morning for the same back-breaking labor.

Let's get something straight. There was nothing wrong with the fact that they were working. Every able-bodied person needs to find some meaningful work to do. God designed us for work. Work was Adam's primary activity in the Garden of Eden. If you are eighteen or older and in good health, get a job. If nobody will hire you, hire yourself. Pay $10.00 for a lawnmower at a yard sale and start mowing people's yards. Think about what you are good at and start doing it. Quit talking about what you can't do. Trade in all that worldly thinking for godly thinking. Deuteronomy 8:18 says that God has given you the ability to produce wealth. Get rid of your stinking thinking. Go to work somewhere doing something and give it your all: "Whatever your hand finds to do, do it with all your might" (Ecclesiastes 9:10).

Parents, teach your children the importance and value of work. Stop coddling them and giving them money for everything. When they are old enough, send them out to get a job. Once they are on their own, they will need job skills and a good work ethic in order to be successful. You don't do them any favors by pampering them.

The Israelites were working hard making bricks and digging ditches. Nothing is wrong with that. However, there *is* something wrong with working hard when one hundred percent of the profit from your sweat and your labor goes to build someone else's empire. In Egypt it was the pharaoh. There are "pharaohs" in our modern day world that many of us slave for, and they go by such names as Visa, MasterCard, Discover, Carte Blanche, Diners Club, and the granddaddy of them all, "Debt."

All the Israelites wanted was a chance to go away for a few days into the wilderness to worship God, but they couldn't because they had a taskmaster over them and they had to work. When Moses made the request of Pharaoh, the Egyptian king responded by increasing the work burden of the people. Before, the Egyptians had provided the people with straw to make the bricks; now, the Hebrews had to find their own straw but still produce the same quota of bricks. Pharaoh was only exercising the "golden rule": He who has the gold makes the rules. As slaves, the Israelites had no rights and no voice.

A lot of you would love to get away for the weekend to go to a marriage retreat, a Promise Keeper's retreat, a youth retreat, a family retreat, or a revival somewhere, but you've got yourself so far in bondage to debt that you can't even take an hour off from trudging around in the mud to go somewhere and get alone with God. You can't go to the wilderness to worship God for three days. Some of you can't even come to church on Sundays because you have to put in mandatory overtime or you need the extra work because you are so far in debt. When someone invites you to a Bible study or asks you to get involved in a particular ministry you say, "Sorry, but I have to work." If this describes you, don't get discouraged about where you are. A day of exit is coming. If you are not in this situation, be careful to avoid it.

The story of Israel's deliverance from slavery in Egypt is told in the book of Exodus. The word *exodus* means, "exit." They exited Egypt and entered freedom. It is time for us to exit stinking thinking about money and enter the Promised Land of financial freedom. What areas in your life would you like to exit? A high mortgage payment? A car payment? Credit card bills with their oppressive interest rates? No longer should we be living in the land of Not Enough. Neither should we simply stand around complacently satisfied in the land of Just Enough. We need to graduate into the land of More Than Enough: more than enough of God, more than enough money, more than enough of everything.

If we are ever going to get to the land of More Than Enough, we have to make an exodus from where we are. For some of you, if you have trouble handling credit cards, it may take "plastic surgery." Credit cards are a fine convenience as long as you can control them. If you can't pay a credit card balance in full when the bill comes, don't use credit cards.

I (Ken) have a walletfull of credit cards, which I use because I earn airline miles. If I can make more money any kind of way, I'll do it. Every month when the bills come, I pay them in full. The credit cards are handier than using cash or writing checks, so I use them when we go on vacation, and the airline miles I have earned make plane tickets a lot cheaper.

Safe use of credit cards requires a lot of discipline. Despite their convenience, credit cards carry another potential risk. Studies show that if you use your credit card to buy your groceries or anything else, even if you pay the bill in full at the end of the month, chances are you will buy more than you would have with cash.

Things have really changed since we were kids. We still remember our parents and others joking that a bank was a place where you could borrow money as long as you could prove that you didn't need it. Credit was hard to get, and if you *did* get it, you had really earned the privilege. It's not that way anymore. Our economy rises or falls on the wave of consumer credit. Today just about anyone can get a credit card. There are even companies that specialize in credit cards for people with bad credit! Go figure.

A few years back the big thing with the credit card companies was to flood college students with opportunities to have their very own credit cards. Thousands upon thousands of students took the bait— and got reeled in like trout. To their everlasting credit, many of those students handled the responsibility well. The sad story is the thousands of others who had to drop out of school, their dreams of a college education—and a well-paying career—shipwrecked on the shoals of debt. They traded their financial freedom for bondage to the "pharaohs" of their world.

In 1995, Sears and Roebuck made more money from interest on their credit cards than they did from the sale of their merchandise. Getting credit is a lot like going to a drug dealer. The first "hit" is free in the hope that you will get hooked and become a regular paying customer. "Your good credit has earned you this credit card. Use it now. No interest until next year." The first "hit" is free. "You can save ten percent now if you sign up for our credit card." If you're not careful, you will get sucked in. When we pay interest on Visa and MasterCard at eighteen, twenty, or twenty-two percent, we are like stock they have invested in. Who can blame them? Wouldn't you give anybody any amount of money if you knew you would get an eighteen- or twenty-percent return every month?

Remember the truth of Proverbs 22:7: "The rich rule over the poor, and the borrower is servant to the lender." Let me tell you something, friends. God will give you favor, and God will open doors for you, but if you want to become financially prosperous, you have to practice godly principles. Slaving away to finance debt is not one of them. Learning how to save your money *is*.

Saving

Why should we save money? Very simply, it is a wise and prudent step to take against the eventuality of famine. As we saw in the last chapter, famine *will* come and we need to be prepared. Cars will break down. Furnaces will go out. Air conditioners will go on the fritz. Spouses will get sick. Women will get pregnant. (Hey, babies cost money! Famine is not always bad, just expensive!) Daughters will get married. Children will go to college. All of these illustrate the need for a sound savings plan, and this is just a short list.

Basically, there are three reasons why we need to save our money. Number one is emergencies. *Money* magazine states that seventy-five percent of all families have a financial tragedy within any given ten-year period of time. We think it is tragic for a Christian to have an emergency and have to beg and borrow to get by. Once isn't so bad, or even twice, but a continual pattern of financial "emergency" is another story. After your friend has paid your rent one month, don't go back to him the next month with the same problem. If you can't afford your rent, either move or cut your spending so you can afford it. If you only make a thousand dollars a month, don't live in an apartment that costs you eight hundred dollars a month. That's just common sense. The point is, emergencies come. We don't know when or where or in what form they will come, but they will come. We need to save money regularly to prepare ourselves for dealing with emergencies.

A second reason for saving our money is that Christians ought to pay cash as much as possible. Paying cash as we go is more responsible, easier to keep track of, and helps us avoid the debt trap. Remember the golden rule of finance, that he who has the gold makes the rules. When we pay cash, we have financial power and generally can get things at a cheaper price. Just avoiding the interest of buying on credit will save hundreds of dollars in the long run.

Consider these two scenarios. First, you want to buy a new car, so you go to the dealer and purchase one for $16,000 and enter into a financing agreement to pay $300 a month for six years. At the end of six years, when your financing is paid off, you will have paid $21,600.00 for a $16,000.00 car that is now six years old and worth perhaps only a fraction of its original value. To top it off, you have no money in the bank to put toward another car. By this time, it may be time to repeat the entire process. This is the "play now, pay later" scenario.

In the second scenario, instead of buying a $16,000 car, you choose a $6,000 car. Instead of paying $300 a month, you pay only $100 a month and place the other $200 in a savings account of some kind or invest it somewhere that will net you a return of around ten percent. If you follow this plan for seven years, your car may be a rattling piece of junk by then, but you also have around $24,000 in the bank. Now you can buy a $16,000 car, pay cash for it, and still have $8,000 in the bank continuing to earn interest. This, of course, is the "pay now, play later" scenario.

Which scenario makes more sense? Our problem is that we don't like to wait and our society drums into our head day after day that we don't have to wait. Saving money works and it makes good sense, but doing it successfully requires commitment, discipline, and patience.

The third reason that we ought to save money is, very simply, to build wealth. Saving money is an awesome way to build wealth because it is based on the principle of multiplication. Let me give a couple of examples to illustrate how this works.

Do you want to know how to retire as a millionaire? There are many ways. Here is one of them. Let's say that you are twenty years old. If you will put just $65.00 a month in some investment that will yield at least a twelve percent return (the average return of stocks in the stock market since 1939 is thirteen percent), and continue doing it for forty years, at the age of sixty, you will have $1,394,000. That's from committing only $65.00 a month, easily the cost of dinner for two at a nice restaurant once a month. Even more amazing is the fact that $65.00 a month for forty years means a total out-of-pocket investment of only

$31,200! All the rest is compounded interest.

With information like this available, no one who is twenty or younger has any excuse for not retiring as a millionaire.

The Value of Starting Early

The second example illustrates the value of starting to save early, the earlier the better.

AGE	BEN INVESTS	BEN HAS	ART INVESTS	ART HAS
22	1,000	1,100	0	0
23	1,000	2,310	0	0
24	1,000	3,641	0	0
25	1,000	5,105	0	0
26	1,000	6,716	0	0
27	1,000	8,487	0	0
28	1,000	10,436	0	0
29	1,000	12,579	0	0
30	0	13,837	1,000	1,100
31	0	15,221	1,000	2,310
32	0	16,743	1,000	3,641
33	0	18,418	1.000	5,105
34	0	20,259	1,000	6,716
35	0	22,285	1,000	8,487
36	0	24,514	1,000	10,436
37	0	26,965	1,000	12,579
38	0	29,662	1,000	14,937
39	0	32,628	1,000	17,531
40	0	35,891	1,000	20,384
41	0	39,480	1,000	23,523
42	0	43,428	1,000	26,975
43	0	47,771	1,000	30,772
44	0	52,548	1,000	34,950
45	0	57,802	1,000	39,545
46	0	63,583	1,000	44,599
47	0	69,941	1,000	50,159
48	0	76,935	1,000	56,275
49	0	84,628	1,000	63,002
50	0	93,091	1,000	70,403

51	0	102,400	1,000	78,543
52	0	112,640	1,000	87,497
53	0	123,904	1,000	97,347
54	0	136,295	1,000	108,182
55	0	149,924	1,000	120,100
56	0	164,917	1,000	133,210
57	0	181,409	1,000	147,631
58	0	199,549	1,000	163,494
59	0	219,504	1,000	180,943
60	0	241,455	1,000	200,138
61	0	265,600	1,000	221,252
62	0	292,160	1,000	244,477
63	0	321,376	1,000	270,024
64	0	353,514	1,000	298,127
65	0	388,865	1,000	329,039

...and Art never caught up !

At age twenty-two, Ben makes the decision to start investing $1,000 a year in a bank or the stock market or in some other vehicle that will earn good interest. Ben's friend, Art, who is also twenty-two, invests nothing. Eight years later, at age thirty, Ben has invested a total of $8,000 but with compounded interest actually has $12,579 in the bank or in stocks. As the chart indicates, even if Ben stops investing at this point and does not put another penny into savings, his original investment of $8,000 will still grow to $388,865 by the time he is sixty-five. Try to imagine how much money Ben would have if he continued to invest the same amount through all those years!

Let's say that Art, who has watched Ben's bank account grow for eight years, decides he had better get busy himself. Beginning at age thirty, Art invests $1,000 a year every year until he turns sixty-five. Look at the difference. Art's out-of-pocket investment is $35,000—more than four times what Ben invested—yet his return at age sixty-five is only $329,039. No matter how long Art continues to invest at the rate of $1,000 a year, he will never catch up to Ben. What made the difference? Ben began saving eight years earlier than Art did.

"But I don't have a thousand dollars to invest!" You probably do. One thousand dollars a year is only $84.00 a month or $19.23 a week. That's less than the cost of dinner for two at an average restaurant, or about the same as the cost of two movie tickets plus popcorn. Saving money is not as much a matter of having the money to save as it is a matter of changing our thinking. We have lived with "I can't" for so long that we fail to consider other alternatives.

Small Change Is Big Money

Small savings can really add up over time. Just $20.00 a week in pizza money, if invested instead in a mutual fund with a nine percent annual return, would be worth a quarter of a million dollars in thirty years. Below is a sampling of a few other common items that are familiar to all of us, their unit and annual costs, and their value if the money was invested instead in a mutual fund such as a 401(k).

ITEM	COST	ANNUAL COST	VALUE IN 2020 IF INVESTED IN A 401(k)
ATM Fees	$2.50 per wk (didn't use your own bank)	$130	$7,280
Soda	$.75 per can 5 times/wk	$195	$10,192
Pedicure	$35.00 sessions 4 times/yr	$210	$11,595
Lottery Tickets	$1.00 per ticket 5 times/wk	$260	$13,302
Frozen Yogurt	$3.00 for a large (with sprinkles) 2 times/wk	$312	$15,962
Cigar	$5.00 per stogie (box of 25) 4 boxes/yr	$500	$25,580
Mocha Latte	$3.00 per grande 5 times/wk	$780	$43,682

Movie Tickets for Two	$20.00 per wk (includes tickets, popcorn and soda)	$1,040	$53,207
Women's Shoes	$70.00 pair 15/yr	$1,050	$53,718
Dinner Out for Two	$50.00 dinner 2 times/wk	$5,200	$291,214

Our point here is not to convince you to stop buying soda or eating out or going to the movies, but to help reorient your thinking to realize that even small amounts of money invested or saved regularly can mean big bucks in the long run. Don't think that you cannot save money because you don't have enough. You may have to make some changes, cut out a few purchases in order to invest the money instead, but you can do it.

Start saving your money. Money invested multiplies. That is a law of economics. It is also a biblical principle of sound money management.

Shifting

As we learn to move from slaving to saving, the day will come when God does some *shifting*. He is going to take the money of the wicked and shift it to the righteous. Accepting this truth will require a shift in our thinking. If God is going to bless us with the money of the wicked, then we have to shift also. We have to start planting some of our seed instead of eating all of our harvest.

Just before the Israelites left Egypt, the Israelite women went to their Egyptian neighbors and asked for their treasures. "Excuse me; we're getting ready to take off, and we'd like to have your gold. We'll need it where we're going." The Bible says the Egyptians gave them gold, silver, and other precious treasures without an argument or a fight. What clearer proof do we need that this was ordained of God? Exodus 12:36 says that the Lord made the Egyptians favorably disposed toward the Israelites, to give them treasures as they asked.

When something is ordained of God, it *will* happen, guaranteed. We believe the same situation applies to God's people today. God has laid up the wealth of the wicked for us. If God has ordained it, He will bring it to pass. When the time is right, a great shift will occur. That is why we must train ourselves to be ready. God wants to shift some of the world's wealth your way, but if you are not ready—if you are like the third investor who buried his talent in the ground—God will shift your portion to someone else. We're not saying that all the rest of the world will become poor while all the Christians become rich. We are saying that God wants to bless us financially so that more of the world's money will go to holy and righteous causes, that more money will be available for the work of the Kingdom of God. We also believe that God's plans for these last days will require that His people in general know how to be good stewards because the great end-time revival that is coming will channel many of the resources of the world into the hands of Christians, and we had better know how to handle them.

That's why we ought to have wealth. That's why God wants us to produce wealth. He doesn't give it to us so that we can consume it selfishly on our own greed, lusts, and desires. If we learn to bless God's Kingdom with what we have, He will give us more. The more we prove ourselves faithful, the more He will invest in us—the more He will entrust to us—until we have so much blessing that we don't have room enough for it.

God invests in us so that we may in turn reinvest in the work of His Kingdom. In doing so, God Himself has set us the highest possible example. After all, He made the greatest investment that has ever been made: "For God so loved the world that he gave his one and only Son, that whoever believes in him shall not perish but have eternal life" (John 3:16). When God invested in us, He invested His very best—His Son—and His investment pays big dividends. All who take His investment receive eternal life. In like manner, we who are the children of God should invest all that we have and are—our lives, our time, our talents, our gifts, and our resources—in the Lord and His work, because he is the owner of all things anyway. When we align our will with His will and our practices with His principles, He will bless us abundantly and, through us, bless others and draw them to Himself. It is truly a win-win situation.

Chapter Twelve

INVESTING FOR SUCCESS

How much are you willing to pay for success? What price can you put on continuing to grow? Throughout this book we have stressed that for Christians, financial management is a spiritual issue and that God is intimately concerned about how we use the financial resources He has given us. We are stewards of His resources, not owners, and He holds us accountable for our stewardship. God wants to bless us financially and in other ways as well, but we must follow His principles if He is to do so. He has given us the ability to produce wealth and expects us to turn a profit. From the beginning, His command to us was to be fruitful and multiply.

Financially speaking, we multiply by learning not to eat all our harvest, but hold back some seed for planting so that we will have future harvests. In other words, we multiply by not spending every penny we get, but allowing our money to grow through giving, as in the tithe and other offerings, and through investing. There is nothing wrong with Christians having money and enjoying nice things and living an affluent lifestyle as long as we keep our priorities in order and serve God and not mammon. One of the ways we do this is by remembering that the purpose of wealth is not for us to consume on our own selfish pleasures and desires, but to invest in the Kingdom of God and in His work.

What specifically does this mean in practical terms? How do we invest in God's Kingdom? We want to try to answer these questions by first looking briefly at our corporate financial responsibility—how a church should use its money. Secondly, we want to present in greater depth four practical areas where we should invest in a personal or individual vein.

Invest in Winning the Lost

Corporately speaking, we need to use our finances to win the lost. The Church of Jesus Christ has no greater priority, no higher mission, than to bring unsaved people into God's Kingdom by leading them to repent of their sins and trust in Jesus Christ as their personal Lord and Savior. Every penny we spend in our churches should, in one way or another, serve that end. If our primary focus is on anything other than reaching the lost for Jesus, we are on the wrong track.

Churches talk a lot about growth. There's nothing wrong with that, provided they seek to grow in order to reach more people and do not seek growth for its own sake. Financially speaking, churches can grow two ways: cheap growth and expensive growth. Cheap growth is reaching people by utilizing existing facilities and resources: Simply open the doors and let them come in. Ministry, outreach, discipleship, and evangelism are all carried out within the existing budget and in accordance with preestablished goals. No "extra" expenditures are involved because everything is covered under operating costs that have already been approved.

When cheap growth works, empty seats are filled and program ministry and support budgets are stretched to the limit. That is when expensive growth must come into play. Once the church is full, it is time to do something different if we want the growth to continue. We may need to expand the parking lot. We may need to go to two services in order to accommodate everyone who comes. This means paying the light bill twice and the air conditioning bill twice because we have to fill up the building twice. Continued growth may require constructing a new building for Sunday school or a new worship center because the old ones are too small. It may require buying more buses to bring new people in as neighborhood outreaches expand. All of these things require money, which is why it is called expensive growth.

Any church that desires to grow must count the cost, literally, and decide whether it is willing to pay the price for growth. Some churches aren't. Either they are content where they are or they are afraid to grow. They may be a self-satisfied "bless-me" club, or perhaps a financial crisis years ago has made them skittish about taking any financial risks. Whatever the case, it is a proven principle that any organization will stop growing when the price of growth gets too high.

For a church trying to reach the lost, how high a price is "too high"? Many of us say we want to go deeper with God until we find out what it will really cost us. The deeper we go with God, the more we have to die to self and the more arrows the enemy shoots our way. For some of us, it is too high a price to pay. "Oh, I didn't realize it involved all of *that!*"

What is the value of one human life? How do you put a price on an unsaved soul for whom Christ died? Our church leadership is determined that in our church the price will never be too high to reach another lost person for Christ. Utility bills, facilities and maintenance costs, staff salaries, and insurance are all necessary expenses for a church, but they are also essential in enabling our church to carry out its primary mission of reaching the lost. Our church likes the slogan "Let's win the lost at any cost." There are many other costs besides just money. There is the cost of increased time spent in expanding ministries, the cost of inconvenience in adjusting to new schedules, and the cost of adapting to change and frequently moving out of our comfort zone to face new challenges. Is it worth the price? Every time we see a new believer immersed in the waters of the baptismal pool, we know the answer. It *is* worth the price, absolutely and without a doubt.

Although we believe that churches ought to be financially prosperous in order to reach the lost more effectively, we do not believe that they should hoard money. God blesses us so we can bless others, and the only way we can bless others is by giving away our blessings. The Church exists for the purpose of fulfilling Jesus' commission to "go and make disciples of all nations, baptizing them in the name of the Father and of the Son and of the Holy Spirit, and teaching them to obey everything I have commanded you" (Matthew 28:19-20a). If that is not our purpose, we might as well close our doors.

Fulfilling the Great Commission is costly, and the cost gets greater the further we go. The higher up the mountain we climb, the more worn-out we become, the colder it gets, and the harder the wind blows. We need to keep the vision before us that we will reach the lost at any cost. Unfortunately, many churches lost that vision years ago. One church of about eight hundred people that we know of had experienced no growth in twelve years, yet had five million dollars sitting in the bank. When asked what they planned to do with all that money, the pastor replied, "We're saving it for a rainy day." What a waste.

What could your church do with five million dollars? Maybe your church *has* five million dollars. What are you doing with it? With five million dollars you could go into the inner city and plant another church. You could open up a youth center or a literacy center, a food bank or a homeless shelter, a career counseling center or free day care—all with a Christ-centered focus aimed at bringing people to the Lord. An evangelist came to our church and said to me, "Pastor, you might as well get used to it. You're going to be in a financial issue the rest of your life, because there will always be someone else to reach with the gospel." There will always be another bus to buy, another outreach ministry to carry out. We can't afford to hoard. Let's use our money to win the lost.

Family

When it comes to personal investing, our money is like seed planted in a field in anticipation of a profitable harvest. With this in mind, let's look at four fertile "soils" in which we should invest. The first of these is the "soil" of *family*. Next to our personal relationship with God, our family is our highest priority. As a matter of fact, our personal spiritual health is directly related to how we care for our family. Paul tells us in 1 Timothy 5:8, "If anyone does not provide for his relatives, and especially for his immediate family, he has denied the faith and is worse than an unbeliever." Our first financial priority is to invest our finances to win our family to Christ and nurture them in their Christian walk.

What are you investing in for your family? "But, you just don't understand. I don't have enough money to send my son to church camp this summer." Why not? You send him to basketball camp every summer. "My kids won't be at Wednesday night youth group for a while. They have softball." What are we teaching our kids when we place greater importance on secular activities (no matter how good) than we do on activities that will help them learn to know and love the Lord? How will they ever learn the value of the things of God if we allow those things to take second place in our priorities and in our spending?

Try being creative when investing in your family. Some of you may pay your children an allowance for taking out the garbage. Why not give them an allowance for reading their Bible every day? That's just a thought. If you're going to reward them for being a garbage man, why not reward them for getting to know God? Perhaps you are always on your kids' backs for listening to secular music. Instead of coming down so hard on their music choices, why not give them twenty bucks and tell them to buy a Christian CD. Any style of popular secular music today has its counterpart in the Christian music scene. They won't have any trouble finding something they like. Send them, or better yet, *take* them to Christian concerts. (Just don't be hurt or surprised if they don't want to hang around with you while you are there).

Take family vacations and plan them in such a way as to include something that will interest everyone. A yearly family vacation is an event that is worth investing much care, prayer, time, and energy into planning so that it will be one of the highlights of the year and create memories that will last a lifetime. Well-planned vacations don't necessarily always have to be expensive, but at the same time, don't settle for a second-class experience just to save money.

Husbands and wives, invest in your marriage. Attend a Christian marriage enrichment seminar together. Plan special weekends for just the two of you to get out of town. Take regular dates together where you don't scrimp on dinner or entertainment.

Invest in your marriage. Invest in your children. Invest your finances back into your home in a way that will be pleasing and glorifying to God. Give priority to those things that are truly important. One family in our church has nine children. They live nearly an hour away, yet those parents are constantly bringing different ones of those kids to events or activities at the church. We sometimes think that they must live on the road. We know it is tough for them, but we thank God that those parents are willing to be inconvenienced for their kids, that they are willing to invest the time and money to make sure their children get into the things of God.

Stewardship is another area where we need to invest in our families. Are you teaching your children how to be good stewards? Do they understand the purpose and importance of tithing? So many children and young people today do not have the foggiest notion about how to manage money. They will drop $150.00 for a new pair of tennis shoes without batting an eye, but have no concept of saving money or setting aside for the future. It is vital that we as Christian parents teach our children to manage money according to God's principles.

One man in our church shared with Ken his approach to teaching his children financial responsibility. I think it is awesome. He gives his children an allowance of one dollar for every year of their age. His method will work for any family. For example, if you have an eight-year-old son and a six-year-old daughter, your son would receive $8.00 every week and your daughter, $6.00. The first thing to teach them is to return to God His share: ten percent comes off the top right away for a tithe. If they want to give a little more, that's fine. Since the tithe on $8.00 is eighty cents, your son might just go ahead and give a dollar. Next, have them set aside fifty percent for a college and career fund. Finally, fifteen percent comes out for a "family tax." When your family goes on vacation, your children's spending money comes out of the family tax. Out of your son's original $8.00 allowance, seventy-five percent has been set aside for one purpose or another, leaving him with $2.00, a reasonable amount for an eight-year-old. On top of everything, he is learning from a very young age to be responsible with money, a skill that will benefit him tremendously throughout his life.

Parents, your children will not become good stewards by accident. You must teach them. Investing in your family is a top priority.

Neighbors

The second "soil" that we ought to invest in is the "soil" of our neighbors. We ought to plant financial seeds of blessing for our neighbors' benefit. We're not talking about "Joe Blow" next door who needs money for another six-pack. Moses came on the scene and said, "Love your neighbor." Jesus took it even further and messed everything up when He said, "Love your enemies." Jesus is always good at messing up our tidy little world, isn't He? He taught us that our neighbor is anyone who crosses our path who has a need. The Good Samaritan invested his own time, energy, resources, and money to help his neighbor, a complete stranger who had fallen victim to brutal robbers and was unable to help himself.

He treated and bandaged the victim's wounds, put him on his own donkey, took him to an inn, paid for his room, and gave the innkeeper extra money to pay for his lodging and any other charges he might incur. Apparently, the Samaritan had to be on his way, but before he left he told the innkeeper, "Any expense you have beyond what I have given you, I will pay you when I return." Probably the only way he could have done that was because he already had a reputation as a man of integrity, a man known for paying his bills in the past.

Like the Good Samaritan, we ought to be able to use our finances to bless our neighbors. That's what God wants us to do, but many of us can't because we are in bondage to our finances. Many of us couldn't be a Good Samaritan if we wanted to because our resources are tied up. If that is true for you, then get to work now seeing how you can free up some of your assets so you can invest in your neighbors. Essentially, it means having resources in reserve, ready to go when a need or opportunity arises. We never know when a "neighbor" will cross our path, so we need to prepare now. Invest in your neighbors. Be prepared to share your blessings. In the process, you might get a chance to share about the God who gave them to you.

The Church and Its Spiritual Leaders

The third "soil" we should invest in is the "soil" of our church and our spiritual leaders. Stated another way, we need to invest in the place where we are being spiritually fed. There is a lot more involved here than just paying the pastor. That's not what I'm getting at. We all need to invest ourselves—our lives, our minds, our bodies, our time, our hearts, and our money—in the local body of believers of which we are a part. Make no mistake, you *need* your local church and your local church needs you. It needs you to be more than just a pew-sitter; more than just a benchwarmer. The Christian life is not a spectator sport. It is a nitty-gritty, in-your-face, knock-down-drag-out contest with a tenacious enemy. Your church cannot afford to have you sitting on the sidelines. As a Christian, you have been called to be right in the middle of the fight.

That is why you need your local church. You need the encouragement and fellowship of a spiritual family that cares about you. You need the spiritual nourishment and refreshing that comes through times of corporate worship, Bible study, and prayer. You need the collective wisdom of the body when you don't know what to do or where to turn. You need a place to be spiritually accountable in a loving and supportive environment so that you can grow steadily in the Lord. You need a place to find shelter, help, and support when famine comes into your life. You need to invest in your church because your church has invested in you. If you are being spiritually fed, you need to return a portion of what you have received as seed for another harvest.

Many believers are more willing to invest in spiritual leaders and ministries that they don't really know than they are to invest in their local church. You'd find amazing the number Christians who don't tithe but are quite willing to send big-time checks to somebody's television ministry. Don't get us wrong; if you support a television or radio ministry somewhere, that's great as long as you are giving your money to God and not to that television personality. There is certainly a place for Christian broadcast media. What I am saying is that supporting such a ministry is no substitute for supporting your own local church. Don't let your own church die on the vine because you are off watering somebody else's field. When it comes to financial support, give your own local church first priority. Let your support for an outside ministry be a supplemental investment.

There is an accountability factor to consider as well. As a steward of God's resources, you are accountable to Him for how you use them. The problem with investing in outside ministries is that nine times out of ten you will never get any kind of accounting of how that ministry spent your money. That may be a thin point if in your heart you are giving to God rather than to a ministry. At the same time, however, wouldn't you rather invest in soil where you know your seed will grow rather than in soil that you are uncertain of?

Whatever else you do, your tithe belongs in your local church. Since it is God's money anyway, don't try to withhold your tithe just because you don't agree with something the preacher said or did or with a decision the church made. A local church is a *community*, a fellowship of believers who work together, even when they don't always agree, to serve the Kingdom of God and lift up the name of Jesus where they are. It is a joint effort. Your church is a body that functions properly only when every member is in place and faithfully working.

Pastors and other spiritual leaders in your church are worthy of your investment and support in prayer and labor as well as in finances. In fact, the Bible commands us to do so:

The elders who direct the affairs of the church well are worthy of double honor, especially those whose work is preaching and teaching. For the Scripture says, "Do not muzzle the ox while it is treading out the grain," and "The worker deserves his wages."

1 Timothy 5:17-18

The word *elders* could also refer to pastors. The elders or pastors who direct the affairs of the church well are worthy of double honor. *Double honor* literally means, "double pay." Faithful and able church leaders, then, are worthy of double pay, which means that a church body has a responsibility to adequately provide for its leaders financially. This is another reason why every member of a local church needs to invest faithfully and regularly in the affairs of the church.

Anyone who receives instruction in the word must share all good things with his instructor.

Galatians 6:6

Although this verse touches on the theme of financial support for church leaders, we believe it speaks mainly to the need of church members to share the burden of ministry with their pastor and other spiritual leaders. Somehow over the years the emphasis in churches changed gradually from the concept of corporate ministry to the concept of pastoral ministry. Many believers today still assume that ministry is the pastor's job, not theirs. This is at odds with the teaching of the New Testament. A pastor's primary responsibility is to toil in the Word of God and the things of God so that He can give the message of God to the people. Taking care of the elderly and the widows and the orphans and seeking to meet practical needs of people on a daily basis are all important, but the pastor should not be doing it.

That was precisely the problem in the sixth chapter of Acts that led the church in Jerusalem to choose the first seven deacons. Those men were selected to coordinate social ministries so that the apostles could devote all their time to prayer and the preaching and teaching of the Word.

Suppose you had an unsaved friend or family member you had been working on for months that you finally persuaded to come to church with you. Now suppose that on that particular Sunday your pastor said, "I've been so busy visiting everybody this week and taking care of administrative and other details that I didn't have time to get alone with God. I don't have a fresh word from God for you today, so let's just pray and go home." That would be tragic, because that might be your friend or relative's only chance to hear the Gospel.

Investing in your church and its spiritual leaders is a mutual transaction. As you invest in them, they invest in you. Your pastor invests himself in the Word of God, spending much time in study and in prayer with God, seeking His face and striving to feel His heart and know His mind so that he can impart to you and the rest of the church what the Lord has spoken to him. On Sunday, he comes into the pulpit and shares what God has revealed, and you receive an abundant return on his investment. At the same time, you have been working and toiling all week teaching school or making business deals or producing on the assembly line—in short, earning a living. When you come together with others of God's people on Sunday, you bring the fruit of your toil with you and share it, and everyone in the church is blessed.

Your pastor needs to be able to spend his time in the presence of God. It's easy to tell if he has not been. Never settle for anything less. If you're going to be sharing your wealth, he'd better be sharing his wealth. Before judging him too harshly, however, take a look at the situation. It may be that he can't spend the time in God's presence that he needs to because he has to pick up the slack from others in the church who are not carrying the ministry of the church as they should. Maybe there is something you can do to help free up your pastor's time so he can do what he is supposed to do. Church life is community life. We must all work together for success, and that means we must all invest mutually in each other.

Missions

The fourth "soil" that we need to invest our finances in is the soil of different countries, the "soil" called *missions*. We have a mandate from Jesus Christ Himself to proclaim the Gospel around the world: "Go and make disciples of all nations" (Matthew 28:19a). Not all of us can go—in fact, not all of us are called to go ourselves—but all of us can help send those who do go. The apostle Paul asked, "How, then, can they call on the one they have not believed in? And how can they believe in the one of whom they have not heard? And how can they hear without someone preaching to them? And how can they preach unless they are sent?" (Romans 10:14-15a).

Remember how I said that the utmost priority of the Church is to reach the lost for Christ? Giving to missions expands and extends our reach in that area by a thousandfold. This side of Heaven we will never know the eternal ramifications of the investment we make in missionary efforts. What we plant will come back to us in greatly multiplied form. This is particularly true with missions giving. Supporting missions is a high-yield investment that keeps on compounding.

Eight Financial Tips

God wants to bless you financially so that you can in turn bless others. He wants you to turn a profit so that whatever you put your hand to will prosper. Do you still have trouble believing it? Remember the story of Joseph in Egypt. By applying God's wisdom, Joseph saved a nation from famine. Egypt had wealth beyond imagination. God blessed even a heathen nation because they used His principles. If God could bless a heathen nation, don't you think He can bless you?

Changing your thinking and behavior regarding finances may seem like a daunting task. It doesn't have to be. Set up a personal plan of action and get started. To help you along, we want to share eight financial tips with you in closing. We chose eight tips because eight is the number of new beginnings. Some of these you have heard before, so let this serve also as a kind of summary review.

1. Educate your ignorance. If you don't know something, ask someone who does. Visit your local library or bookstore. Both should have any number of books on finances and financial management. If you don't like to read, get tapes. Attend financial seminars, especially ones hosted by a church. They are usually free and will present financial principles from a godly and biblical perspective. Sit down and talk to someone you trust who has succeeded in the area of financial management. Search the Internet. All the information you need is out there. There is no shame in *being* ignorant but there is shame in *staying* ignorant when you don't have to. Educate your ignorance.

2. Start saving today. No matter what your situation, put something aside regularly for savings, even if it is only five dollars a week. Establishing the discipline to save is the hardest part of the battle.

3. Put your money to work. Stop focusing on spending and start focusing on investing.

4. Protect yourself and your assets. Start laying up resources to protect against unexpected trouble—the famines of life. Be sure to carry sufficient life, health, automobile, and homeowner's insurance. Take care of your health.

5. Do not pay interest on credit cards or unnecessary banking fees. You are a consumer. Shop around for a bank that will you give you the best services at the lowest rates. Don't use credit cards unless you can pay the balances in full each month.

6. Live below your income. Follow the 10-10-80 plan: pay God ten percent, pay yourself ten percent, and live on eighty percent. Never spend money that you do not have, not even money that you fully expect to receive. If your boss has promised you a Christmas bonus, don't spend it until you actually have it. If you don't have it in time for Christmas, don't splurge. Wait until later and take advantage of the after-holiday sales. Don't increase your level of spending just because you get a pay increase. The biggest cause of financial problems is uncontrolled spending.

7. Utilize the savings vehicles of your company. If your employer offers a 401(k) or similar savings and retirement plan, take full advantage of it. Since most plans include employer matching funds, make sure you contribute enough to qualify for full employer matching.

8. If no one will hire you, hire yourself. It is the silliest thing to be in America and say, "I can't get a job." When I (Ken) first came to Michigan, I had no plans to stay. I was on vacation, but then I met a beautiful young woman who later became my wife. All of sudden, I realized that I needed money. I opened a business. I hired myself. I went to a bank and asked, "Who cleans your building?" They said, "It's funny you should ask, because we just fired a cleaning company because we were disappointed in their work and are looking for a replacement." I said, "Let me have the job. I will do whatever you need." I did the same at a local gym. I went out and bought a vacuum cleaner and a bottle of Windex and went to work. I supported myself for a while that way. If no one will hire you, hire yourself.

Following God's principles of financial management will change your life. They will help you get out of debt and begin turning a profit, even if you never thought it could happen. Be faithful with the tithe, honor God with your other ninety percent, and He will turn your situation around. It probably won't happen overnight, but He will bring it to pass. Give generously and experience Jesus' promise: "Give, and it will be given to you. A good measure, pressed down, shaken together and running over, will be poured into your lap. For with the measure you use, it will be measured to you" (Luke 6:38). Learn to stop spending and start investing. God is looking for a good return on His investment. Be faithful with a little and He will give you more. Set your heart on the goal to hear Him say to you:

"Well done, good and faithful servant! You have been faithful with a few things; I will put you in charge of many things. Come and share your master's happiness!" Matthew 25:21

CHAPTER THIRTEEN

LOOKING BACK, LOOKING AHEAD

Although the main thrust of this book is on the personal level, we felt it would be helpful to look briefly at the societal level for a larger perspective. We believe that in order to put our individual financial puzzle pieces in place we need to see where we fit within the overall picture of the financial world. The lack of understanding of money and its functions lies at the root of many of our societal as well as personal problems.

Money traditionally serves three basic functions in society: 1) means of exchange; 2) standard of value; 3) measurement of worth. Understanding why and how each of the functions evolved is helpful in understanding how money affects our personal lives today and in the future. To get a perspective on money's evolution, we need to look at its development through history.

The Historical Perspective

The history of money begins with people learning to trade the things they had for the things they wanted. If they wanted a candle, they had to find someone who had one and who was willing to exchange it for their ax, for example. This system is obviously cumbersome and limiting. It takes time and energy to find someone with exactly what you want or need who is also willing to take what you have to offer. And it isn't easy to agree on the value of those things. How many skins is an ax worth? Or how many beads is a piece of land worth? What happens if the cow you want is worth an ax and a half? As trade flourished, money came into existence as a means of exchange to solve some of these issues.

Over time, a "market" would develop which would fix a value of each item relative to another. For instance, one ax would be "equal" to five candles, and a candle might be "worth" two apples. Once buyers and sellers agreed what was acceptable as the amount of payment, they then established a system with different values for coins (or other items they would consider as money).

Using money also meant that buying and selling did not have to happen at the same time. This allowed for the development of wealth creation because people could accumulate money from a number of sales to give them more buying power.

Money has taken many forms over the years. As children, we learned that the Indians sold the Dutch the island of Manhattan for twenty-four dollars' worth of beads and trinkets. In Rome, soldiers were often paid with sacks of salt, which in Latin is *sal*, the root for our word *salary*. In the Solomon Islands, the people use tobacco, as they do in our prison system, for personal transactions.

Throughout the centuries, thousands of different items, from palm branches to coffee beans to precious metals, have served as money. The Bible lists items from grain to olive oil, although by the time of Exodus various precious metals (gold, silver, and copper were among them) were being used to pay for goods and services in Egypt and Asia Minor. By 700 BC, the Kingdom of Lydia was minting coins made of a substance called electrum, a pale yellow alloy of gold and silver. The coins were valuable, durable, and portable. Better yet, they couldn't die or rot on the way to market. Gold and gold coins were such a crucial part of the ancient world that one of the biggest occupations was alchemy. *Alchemy* is defined by Webster's New College Dictionary as "the medieval chemical science that was to change base metals into gold; to transform something common into something precious." Paul Zane Pilzer has written exhaustively about a subject he refers to as "economic alchemy." He writes, "The ancient alchemists sought to discover the secret of turning base metal into gold; how to create great value where little existed before. They believed that by discovering how to make gold they could obtain unlimited prosperity for all of God's children.... Their faith in the eventual success of their quest was guided by their faith in a true and just God—for such a God could not have created a world where the only way to get gold, or wealth, was to take it from someone else."

The other development that came with the use of coins is that coins could be counted as opposed to being weighed. Obviously, this simplified the exchange process even more. It also allowed for a geographical dispersion of commerce. No longer did all transactions need to be conducted at the market. Now you could sell your broom, ax, or cow in the next town.

Historians have found that the Babylonians had the idea of paper money as early as 2500 BC in the form of receipts and bills. The earliest bills can be traced to China. There is evidence that Kublai Khan issued paper notes made from mulberry bark bearing his seal and his treasurers' signatures in 1282. The first European bank notes were printed in Sweden in 1661, and France put paper money into circulation in the 1700's. In the British Empire, paper money was first issued in the form of promissory notes given to Massachusetts soldiers in the late 1600's when their siege of Quebec failed and there was no booty with which to pay them. This idea became popular with other colonies, if not with the soldiers who were paid that way.

The history of the dollar can be traced to a silver coin called the Joachimsthaler that was minted in 1519 in the valley of Saint Joachim in Bohemia. This coin, for reasons that are still debated, was widely circulated through Holland, Scandinavia, and England. More than twenty countries besides the United States call their currency "dollars."

The U.S. dollar's early history was best described as chaotic until the National Banking Act of 1863 established a uniform currency. Before that, banks used paper money, but they couldn't always meet their customers' demands for hard currency, whether it be gold or silver coins. At that time, the dollar was often exchanged for just a fraction of its stated value. The National Banking Act brought consistency and objectivity to the U.S. currency and economy. The average American had the benefit of an easily transferable, durable and valuable commodity. There was also a downside. Because it was transferable, durable, and valuable and the banking system had not yet developed fully, US history records the exploits of Jesse James and others who took advantage of paper currency.

Money, as we now know, has evolved from gold, olive oil, firewood, etc., to the government-issued currency of today. Throughout their development, the United States and other countries have experienced trials and tribulations in managing this valuable commodity. Paul Zane Pilzer writes, "Throughout its early existence, the United States was plagued by financial panics that occurred whenever large numbers of people attempted to turn their bank deposits into currency. After the severe panic of 1907, debate ensued on the question of establishing a central bank to regulate banking and the supply of money, and the Federal Reserve System was created in 1913."

The present banking and economic system has developed to be the most powerful in the world. This efficiency, though, has a cost. Most Americans have probably read the books or have seen the movies about Robin Hood. I (Nick) remember as a kid wanting a bow and arrow so I could pretend to be Robin Hood. In some way, it always seemed so romantic and noble to rob from the rich and give to the poor. We as Christians have the responsibilitiy to give to the poor, but robbing from the rich has become a divisive political issue in our society. And although Robin Hood and his merry men are long gone, his followers are still with us today. How often do we hear that the rich have the responsibility to pay for those "less fortunate" in the form of more taxes? Taxes are one of the biggest expenses, if not *the* biggest, that American families face. How many times have we looked at our paychecks and wondered where all the money went *before* we deposited or cashed it? The issue is not one of getting mad about it, but one of getting smart about it. If we don't learn how to manage our money, our money will manage us.

The Societal Perspective

We briefly looked at where money came from historically, but the real question is, how does that impact me today and, maybe more importantly, tomorrow? A wise man once said, "He who does not learn from the past is condemned to relive it." We believe that there are two dimensions to how the history of money impacts us today. The first dimension is on a personal level. One of the personal challenges is to better define the difference between our needs and our wants. This issue was identified over forty years ago by the great economist and Nobel laureate John Kenneth Galbraith, who said, "In the affluent society, no sharp distinction can be made between luxuries and necessities." We are responsible for our own financial destinies. So we need to ask ourselves some questions. Are you satisfied with where you are financially? Where will you be in twenty or thirty years by following the financial practices you have today? Are there things you can be doing better? Do you know how to improve your financial situation?

Some clues to resolving these types of questions can be found in looking at the second dimension, which is societal. What trends do we see that are shaping our collective economic future? The two largest trends that we see facing our country as they relate to money are 1) the impact of the baby boom generation; and 2) the impact of electronic money. For our purposes, we want to look specifically at the first trend. How does the baby boom generation affect us as a society?

Many of us have heard of or are part of the baby boom. In the period between 1946 and 1965, the birthrate in this country almost doubled. The generation born during these years is referred to as the baby boomers. The impact of this generation was and will be felt for years to come.

The size of this portion of our population is causing serious financial repercussions in many ways, but one way in particular that affects each of us individually is in the area of retirement. For generations before the baby boom, the traditional retirement plan consisted of three components: Social Security, company pensions, and savings. Add to those three one more recent component—investments—and you have the financial picture of most baby boomers.

Due to the large onslaught of American baby boomers who will be retiring in the next few years, the future of social security is now dire. The generations that followed the baby boom will be the people who are paying into the social security system as older fellow tax payers retire, and there simply aren't enough of them to support the number of seniors in the baby boom. To top it off, most studies indicate that this generation will live longer, requiring more income for a longer period of time.

Also, large numbers of retirees make company pensions more and more a benefit that corporations can no longer afford, and actually, companies are beginning to cut back on promised benefits. So that leaves investments and savings to cover our needs and expenses when we reach our golden years. The financial markets, however, have also felt the impact of the size of this generation. Over the past five to ten years, nearly one trillion dollars has flowed into the market through mutual funds and equities. However, the majority of our seniors are not doing well financially—only three percent are financially independent. *Money* magazine recently conducted a mutual fund IQ test and less than twenty percent of those who took it passed. This indicates that many people simply don't understand the market. Since we tend to learn the handling of finances from our parents, we may very well be going down a path that will take us where we don't want to be later on. We need to understand the market and the trends in order to make necessary adjustments. Without knowledge, making investments is risky at best and disastrous at worst.

That leaves only savings, but statistics show that the savings rates of Americans have dropped from ten percent in the previous generation to under two percent in this one. We've become a nation of spenders instead of savers. Our ignorance of money matters will be our undoing if we don't learn to stop the slide and begin to operate under biblical principles.

It is our belief that the solution to our problems rests in the three keys outlined in the ROADS diagram showing principle, perception, and practice. It is imperative to learn God's financial and economic rules. We must learn to perceive differently about the use and function of money and our handling of it. We must begin to practice new disciplines to adhere to God's system, and possibly seek the assistance of a professional when we are unable to learn on our own.

The ROADS Illustration

Our illustration of roads depicts four different aspects of our search for financial understanding and freedom. The first component is the GAP that lies between where we are in our financial situations and where we want to be. It seems to be a universal condition that there is a financial GAP in our lives. We see financial success as a destination and a position to attain. God sees our lives in all aspects as a journey. We should view all areas of our lives, including finances, as a journey and not a place of being.

The second aspect of the model is the puzzle at the top. Many of us see finances as a complicated, unintelligible mass of information and

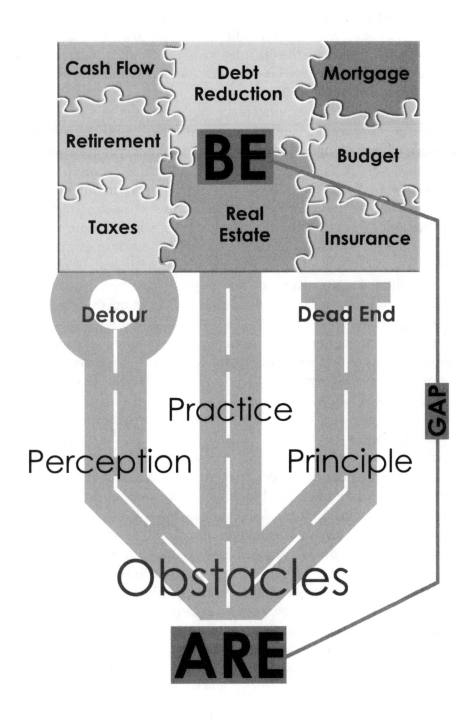

words that we don't understand or comprehend. Financial people have their own language, their own definitions, their own statistics, etc., and we laypeople are on the outside looking in. There appears to be a wall surrounding the sacred keys to financial success and we don't have the password, or so we believe.

The third aspect of the model is the roads themselves. Our perception is that some know a "secret" road, or shortcut, while the rest of us are stalled by challenges such as detours, dead ends, or construction zones.

We are convinced that almost anyone can reduce their financial stress and narrow the GAP by examining the three obstacles (the fourth aspect): Perception, Practice, and Principle. Perception is our view of the world. This includes our view of ourselves, our money, our successes, our failures, our hopes, and our fears. Unfortunately, many of us start with a deficit because of how we view ourselves. In a spiritual sense, we give the devil a foothold that he doesn't need because we are doing his work on ourselves. As it relates to money, many of us need to change our perception from letting our money manage us to managing our money. To be successful in this area requires us to take control of our lives, to refuse to be victims, and to decide to change our destinies for ourselves and our families.

Principles are ideas that we live by that make up our main beliefs. Hopefully, these principles are biblically based. With the exception of salvation, there are more scripture verses about money and wealth than there are about any other topic in the Bible. This is a time, as never before, to be knowledgeable about God's economic system. God's financial principles for a stable economy do not fluctuate; however, the world's economic system changes from day to day. Unfortunately, the Church has not done a very good job of educating its people about these principles and in some cases has taught erroneously.

God's principles were given to bless His people even in the midst of economic turmoil and uncertainty. Genesis 26 tells us the story of Isaac, who was blessed even in the midst of a natural famine because he knew and adhered to God's principles.

The key to success in every area of our lives, including finances, is found in Joshua 1:8.

Do not let this Book of the Law depart from your mouth;
meditate on it day and night, so that you may be careful to do
everything written in it. Then you will be prosperous and
successful.   Joshua 1:8

Finally, practice. Practice is what behavior you engage in. It is our view that practice should be the result of sound principles and perceptions. Harry Truman once said that he preferred "imperfect action to perfect inaction." Some of the principles that should be practiced and that we have described in this book are tithing, learning to pay yourself, getting out of debt, and investing in yourself and your knowledge of finance. Obviously, having all the knowledge and doing nothing with it is useless.

Ironically, we live in a time with more information at our fingertips than ever before. The irony is that we have a society that has more bankruptcies, more debt, and more financial stress than any generation that has come before it. Economic uncertainty, layoffs, corporate scandals, stock market losses, excessive credit card debt, inability to save for the future, stress, overload, relationships in turmoil, too many choices, and wrong priorities all affect our financial situations and have Americans feeling stressed as a result.

Although we are more prosperous as a nation than ever before, the personal financial trends that are sweeping our country and this generation are sobering. Fortunately, there is hope and it is found in God's Word. By applying basic biblical principles to our finances, we can redeem what we have allowed the enemy and our ignorance to steal from us. It is our hope and prayer that *The Morality of Money* will help you develop a plan, train you to manage your money, and chart your course for your life, your finances, and your giving! Then in all things you can truly say, as Joshua said:

But as for me and my household, we will serve the LORD.
                                    Joshua 24:15b